Roses
~ for
# British
# Columbia

Brad Jalbert
Laura Peters

LONE
PINE

Lone Pine Publishing

The Publisher: Lone Pine Publishing
10145 – 81 Avenue
Edmonton, AB T6E 1W9
Canada
Website: http://www.lonepinepublishing.com

National Library of Canada Cataloguing in Publication Data
Peters, Laura, 1968–
    Roses for British Columbia / Laura Peters, Brad Jalbert.

    Includes index.
    ISBN 1-55105-261-X

    1. Rose culture—British Columbia. I. Jalbert, Brad, 1965– II. Title.
SB411.5.C3 P47 2003   635.9'33734'09711   C2002-911162-5

Editorial Director: Nancy Foulds
Project Editor: Shelagh Kubish
Editorial: Shelagh Kubish, Dawn Loewen
Illustrations Coordinator: Carol Woo
Photo Editor: Don Williamson
Production Coordinator: Jennifer Fafard
Book Design: Elliot Engley, Heather Markham
Cover Design: Gerry Dotto
Layout & Production: Curtis Pillipow, Elliot Engley, Heather Markham,
    Arlana Anderson-Hale, Jeff Fedorkiw, Lynett McKell, Ian Dawe
Illustrations: Ian Dawe

Photography: All photographs by Tamara Eder or Robert Ritchie except Agriculture Canada p. 157; Saxon Holt p. 111, 179, 195a, 195b; Brad Jalbert p. 165a, 165b, 183a, 226a, 226b, 257, 260, 261; Liz Klose p. 18a, 36a, 58, 59, 65, 68, 69, 70; Norman Lightfoot p. 16b; Laura Peters p. 34, 39, 40, 47; Don Williamson p. 31, 87.

Front and back cover photographs by Tamara Eder.

Hardiness zones map ©Her Majesty the Queen in Right of Canada, 2002. Reproduced with the permission of the Minister of Public Works and Government Service, 2002.

We acknowledge the financial support of the Government of Canada through the Book Publishing Industry Development Program (BPIDP) for our publishing activities.

PC: P4

CONTENTS

ACKNOWLEDGMENTS

We gratefully acknowledge all who were involved in this project. Thanks to the provincial and municipal rose societies and gardening clubs for their sound advice and direction. We appreciate the work of the primary photographers, Tamara Eder and Robert Ritchie. Thanks to the many beautiful public and private gardens and garden centers that provided the setting for photographs in this book. Special thanks are extended to the following: Adamson's Heritage Nursery, American Rose Society, David Austin Roses Ltd., Brentwood Bay Nurseries, International Rose Test Garden (Oregon), Canadian Rose Society, Tony and Milton Castelino, Centennial Rose Garden (Coquitlam), Campbell G. Davidson, Robert Harkness, Humber Nurseries, Ladd's Rose Garden (Oregon), Peninsula Park Rose Garden (Oregon), Rambling Rose B&B, Claude Richer and Salisbury Greenhouses.

Many thanks to Lone Pine Publishing for giving me the opportunity to work on this exciting book project. Special thanks to Laura Peters for her excellent research and guidance through my first book experience. I have learned a great deal as a member of the Vancouver Rose Society, and I owe a particular thanks to two of the society's former presidents: Janet Wood and Brenda Viney, who have cheered my hybridizing efforts and shared their rose knowledge. Thanks to George Mander, my friend and colleague who has been a great inspiration. His willingness to share his vast knowledge, enthusiasm and love of roses has enabled me to become the rose hybridizer and grower I am today. I owe my career to my mother and father. I was able to develop my passion for roses into a lifelong career based on their steadfast support, hard work and encouragement. To them I give my most humble thanks. —*Brad Jalbert*

I would like to thank my parents, Gary and Lucy Peters, for their love and support and my friends for their endless encouragement. It would have been impossible to begin this project without Don Williamson or complete it without Shelagh Kubish. Thanks to the entire Lone Pine team and to the growers and breeders, rosarians, gardeners and garden centers who shared information, advice and wisdom with me. A special thanks to Paul Barden. I would especially like to thank Brad Jalbert for his knowledge, hard work and sense of humor. —*Laura Peters*

INTRODUCTION

A mong the most beautiful plants to grow, roses reward the gardener in many
ways. Thought by many to be demanding and difficult, roses can in fact
grow almost anywhere with the right combination of sun, water and care. This
book showcases 144 of the best roses for British Columbia gardens and
contains all the information you need to get growing.

Ispahan

There is a beautiful rose for every hardiness zone in British Columbia.

Both ecologically and climatically, British Columbia is the most diverse region of Canada. All nine temperature zones defined by Agriculture Canada can be found here. The climate varies so much because the topography is diverse and because of the influence of the Pacific Ocean. The most important elements of British Columbia's climate are precipitation and temperature. Other factors that affect climate throughout the province include elevation, latitude, air flow and whether a location is coastal or inland.

The west coast rainforest extends along the cool, rainy, west-facing mountainsides and along the length of Vancouver Island. Technically the warmest area of the province, it is the most hospitable to plants that retain their foliage all year, as well as winter-flowering plants. Most roses grow very successfully in this area because of the long, mild growing

Morden Ruby

season and an extraordinary amount of annual sunlight hours. Victoria has an average of 287 frost-free days a year and more than 2100 hours of sunlight a year. The lower mainland isn't far behind, with Vancouver averaging 216 frost-free days and an average of 1900 sunlight hours per year. Vancouver receives most of its precipitation as rain, an average of 1113 mm annually. Winters along the coast are cloudy and wet. Very little snow falls on the coast, especially in the south.

The Gulf Islands have a drier climate because they lie in the rainshadow of the mountains on Vancouver Island and the Olympic Peninsula. The Gulf Islands experience more sunshine than almost any other place in Canada.

Compared to the coast, the interior of British Columbia has a hotter, drier summer, a more clearly defined spring and fall and a colder winter. Some parts of the southern interior are moist, with coast-like vegetation but greater temperature extremes. The summers are particularly hot in the south, including an area encompassing the communities of Lytton, Oliver and Osoyoos, which are often western hot spots, reaching temperatures higher than 86° F (30° C).

The western portion of the southern interior is dry because it is in the rainshadow of the Cascade Mountains. The Okanagan Valley receives only 250 mm of precipitation annually. The eastern portion of the southern interior receives more precipitation.

Madame Hardy

Royal Sunset

Hardiness Zones Map

The north-central interior of the province is fairly rainy (Prince George receives an average 628 mm of precipitation a year), colder in winter and not as hot in summer. This area has a short growing season and very cold winters with reliable snow coverage. Annual snowfall is an average 400 cm or more in the north, including Revelstoke. In the interior, winter cold is broken up by periodic mild Pacific storms that work their way through the mountains.

The climate of the northeast corner of the province is basically an extension of the continental prairie climate. This region experiences warm summers, an extended frost-free period during the growing season but the coldest temperatures of the province. This region also receives more winter sunshine than coastal areas.

Garden conditions can be adapted to meet roses' requirements. Soil can be made lighter or heavier; exposure to wind can be increased or decreased by careful plant placement; soil fertility or pH can be altered; inadequate rainfall can be supplemented by irrigation; excess rainfall can be partially compensated for by improving the drainage. Roses that are tender for a region can be protected with mulch or by hilling.

The B.C. gardener is supported by an active and hospitable gardening population. Outstanding rose shows, public gardens, arboretums and show gardens throughout the province are sources of inspiration as well as information. The roses are usually labeled so you know what to buy if you want to try something in your own garden.

Local and provincial rose societies are useful for all rose gardeners, from the beginner to the enthusiast. Many B.C. gardeners have a detailed knowledge of planting and propagation methods, skill in identifying specific roses and plenty of passionate opinions on what is best for any patch of ground (see Resources, p. 262).

Royal William

Open yourself to the possibilities and you will be surprised by the diversity of roses that thrive in British Columbia's varied climates. Don't be afraid to try something different or new. Gardening with roses is fun and can be a great adventure if you're willing to take up the challenge. When the right rose is chosen for the right location and purpose, you should experience the least resistance and the best success. If your gardening efforts fail, try again. Keep in mind that gardening is discovery, and without discovery there would be little beauty.

Rosemary Harkness

Roses in History

B ritish Columbia rose gardeners today continue a long and venerable tradition of growing and enjoying these plants. Fossil evidence suggests roses flourished up to 32 million years ago; people have been cultivating roses for about 5000 years. Three roses—the gallica, alba and damask—are among the most ancient cultivated plants still grown today.

The ancient Romans used rose petals for medicine, perfume, garlands and wedding confetti. Roses were even consumed in puddings and desserts. Roman nobility sponsored large public rose gardens. Cleopatra covered the floors of her palace in a deep layer of fresh rose petals, and the sails of her barge were soaked in rose water. Rose water also flowed through the emperor's fountains, and pillows were stuffed with petals.

The use of rose oil—which can be found in cosmetics, perfumes and aromatherapy—began in ancient Persia. When it was discovered that rose water lasted indefinitely once bottled, people no longer had to surround themselves with bushels of roses for the wonderful fragrance; they merely had to open a bottle of

William Lobb

rose water or the pure essential oil, also known as attar of roses.

Early Christians associated roses with pagan rites and the excesses of the Romans. Any personal indulgence was considered sinful—including the ancient Roman practice of bathing in water scented with rose oil—and roses fell out of favor. Nevertheless, during the sixth century, St. Benedict planted a little rose garden, or Roseta, which became the model for monastic rose gardens through the Middle Ages. If not for the monastic gardens, some of the ancient roses might have died out.

In the 17th century, roses and rose water were in such demand that they could be used as legal tender to barter or make payments. In France, Napoleon transported gallons of violet and rose scents on his campaigns. It is said that during the Napoleonic Wars, ships carrying roses for Empress Josephine were given free and safe passage. Josephine's rose

Rosa Mundi

Emperor Nero had a party room with a painted ceiling resembling the heavens, which opened up, sprinkling perfume and flowers on the guests. At one such party, guests were said to have been smothered to death by the enormous quantity of rose petals that fell from the heavens.

Reine des Violettes

The ancient Greeks considered rose water more valuable than its weight in gold. The Roman Catholic Church used rose petals to make the beads for rosaries, hence the name.

garden, created in the late 18th century at Malmaison, contained every rose known to exist at that time.

The Victorians of the late 19th century were charmed by the rose, and roses began to appear in poetry and prose, representing virtue and innocence. The form of the modern rose garden, with its symmetry and well-spaced plants, arose in the 19th century.

Stanwell Perpetual

Roses decorated the crests of kings and princes in the 15th-century 'Wars of the Roses' between rivals for the English throne. The white rose symbolized the House of York, and the red rose symbolized the House of Lancaster.

A formal rose garden

The magnificent beauty of roses continues to inspire poetry, paintings and fragrances. Roses are still bred at an astonishing rate, with over 20,000 cultivated varieties in existence. It's hard to imagine a day without roses, without their sweet fragrance and beauty, medicinal and practical uses and all these flowers represent. Roses are a wonderful part of our history and will no doubt always be a part of our future.

William Lobb

Tournament of Roses

A Greek legend attributes the creation of the rose to Flora, the goddess of spring and flowers. She found the lifeless body of one of her beautiful nymphs in the forest and asked the gods to give the creature new life by transforming her into a flower, one that surpassed all others in beauty. The request was granted, and the new flower was named Rose, Queen of Flowers.

Hénri Martin

Anatomy & Rose Terminology

G etting to know the parts and names associated with the rose is a good place for beginners to start. With a little practice you'll be speaking like a seasoned rosarian.

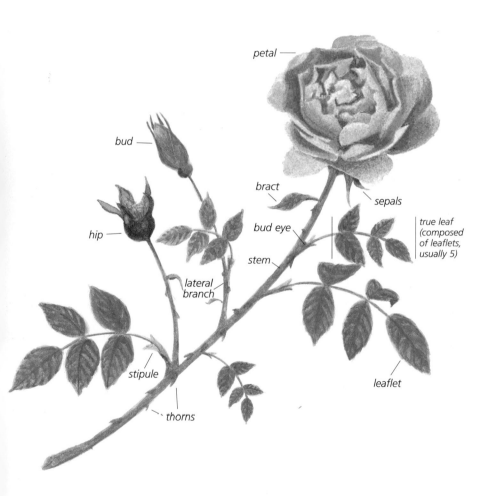

stamens

bract

bud

A species rose

canes

bud union

sucker

A rose root

roots

Roses in the Garden

Landscape Uses

Woody plants—trees and shrubs—are the foundation of your landscape. Roses are flowering shrubs and can be used in any situation that calls for a shrub. Roses can even substitute for annuals and perennials in planting beds. Choose a rose that will work well in the situation you want to use it in. When choosing a rose for a certain purpose or location, consider its hardiness, disease resistance, height and spread, maintenance requirements, growth habit, flowering form and color. The following are landscape situations in which roses can be used to good effect.

BEDS

Rose beds can be formal or informal. Formal rose beds are laid out in precise, geometric patterns that allow the maximum number of rose plants to fit in the beds. Roses are chosen for their upright growth habit and uniform height. Variation in height is added by using standard, or tree, roses. Formal rose beds are suitable for large gardens and cut-flower gardens. Formal gardens may also use roses as accents or features rather than devoting the entire beds to them. A drawback to formal rose gardens is the increased potential for pest and disease outbreaks because the roses are so close together.

Informal rose beds have no precise layout and often include other plants. The choice of which rose to use is limited only by your imagination.

A formal rose bed of Golden Girls

Niagara Parks Rose Garden

Informal style is good for border plantings. Planting roses, or any plants, in odd numbers will help create an informal, natural character.

HEDGES

Roses can be grown as informal (non-manicured) hedges using one or two rows of plants. Hedges using two rows often have a staggered arrangement. Species and shrub roses, especially those that sucker, make good rose hedges. The suckers make the hedge thicker from the bottom up. Rose hedges make excellent barriers as they are nearly impenetrable once established. Do not plan to have a highly manicured rose hedge, as roses do not respond well to being sheared.

Informal planting in mixed bed

GROUNDCOVERS

If you have areas that need some color but are hard to plant or maintain, try low-growing or trailing roses. Trailing roses make the best groundcovers. They look good draping over retaining walls or steep slopes. Roses with dense growth can be effective for weed suppression. Try to begin with an area that is free of weeds for the best result.

Hedge

COVERING AND MASKING

Climbing, rambling and larger shrub roses can be used to cover structures such as pergolas, archways, fences, arbors, posts and buildings. Climbers and ramblers require a supporting structure solid enough to handle the weight of their flower-laden canes. It is best to choose a

Groundcover

Handel trained on a trellis

Mary Rose

Beauty Secret

structure that won't require any maintenance, such as painting, over time because it can be tedious to unwind and detach the shoots from the support only to have to reattach the shoots again.

ACCENTS

Beautiful roses, with their bright colors and wonderful fragrance, are useful accent plants, drawing attention to themselves and away from less attractive parts of your garden.

CONTAINERS

Roses grown in containers, such as planters and hanging baskets, can be used on a deck or balcony or in the garden. They bring the flowers and fragrance close to outdoor sitting areas where they can be enjoyed, and they are a good choice if space is limited. Miniature, polyantha and floribunda roses work well in containers. Standard roses are often grown in containers with shallow-rooted bedding plants. Containers can be used anywhere the growing conditions are right for good rose performance. Containers can be moved to a sunny position and then moved again for winter storage.

Rose Features

Before you go out rose buying, familiarize yourself with some of the different features and classes of roses. This book is divided into nine sections according to the class of each rose. Each section begins with an explanation of the characteristics of the class. The sections are species, old garden, shrub, groundcover, climbers and ramblers, hybrid tea, floribunda, grandiflora and miniature.

CLASSIFICATION

Classifying roses is complex considering there are approximately 150 species and over 20,000 varieties and cultivars. Classification is becoming more difficult as rose hybridizing continues and hybridizers select breeding parents from a large number of possible candidates. Different groups of rosarians have tried to develop systems of classification that encompass all roses. The American Rose Society (ARS) recognizes 55 official classes, the British Association Representing Breeders recognizes 30 official classes and the World Federation of Rose Societies recognizes 39 official classes. In 1971, delegates to the World Rose Convention adopted a system dividing all roses into climbing and non-climbing classes and then further dividing them into recurrent and non-recurrent bloomers.

Adding to the complexity is that different groups classify roses for different purposes. Scientists classify roses according to the botanical characteristics of the flower and plant. The ARS classification system is most useful to those who exhibit roses in competitions. Nurseries and garden centers classify roses according to their growth habit and use in the landscape, a classification system most practical for the average rose gardener.

FRAGRANCE

One of the most important features of roses is the fragrance. The smell of a rose can reach you long before you see the plant. The fragrances can be sweet, spicy, fruity,

The fragrant Double Delight

Fragrant Cloud

musky or one of many other wonderful aromas. The petals usually produce the scent, but the leaves, stems and thorns may also be fragrant. For example, in the moss roses, the fragrance comes from the hairs that cover the stems and bottoms of the flowers.

Many of the modern varieties, such as the hybrid teas and floribundas, have little or no scent at all. It is difficult to retain the scent in the hybridizing process. On the other hand, some of the most intense scents come from the modern varieties. Double Delight and Fragrant Cloud, for example, combine superb flower form and color with a strong fragrance. The English roses bred by David Austin Roses Ltd. (also known as Austin roses) combine rich, heady scents of the once-blooming antique and old garden roses with the repeat blooming of the modern varieties.

Double Delight petals can change to red over time.

Double flowers generally have more fragrance than single flowers, and darker-colored flowers are said to have a stronger fragrance than lighter-colored blooms. The healthier the plant, the more intense the fragrance. The fragrance is strongest on bright, warm sunny days when the air is a little humid and the wind is light. The aroma is reduced on cloudy days and close to undetectable on rainy days. The best time to enjoy the aroma is when the blooms are just opening in the early morning, which is when roses are picked for the perfume industry.

Some of the older classes of roses such as damasks, gallicas and bourbons have rich, complex aromas and are worthy of growing for this reason alone. If you want a fragrant rose, a good choice would be any of those listed at right and on the next page.

Abraham Darby

MOST FRAGRANT ROSES

Abraham Darby
Adélaïde d'Orléans
Beauty Secret
Blanc Double de Coubert
City of London
City of York
Compassion
Constance Spry
Cuthbert Grant
Double Delight
Duchesse de Montebello
Fragrant Cloud
Hébé's Lip
Hénri Martin
Henry Hudson
Henry Kelsey
Iceberg
J.P. Connell
John Cabot
Lavender Lassie
Rosa Mundi
Rosa virginiana
Royal Sunset
Seagull
Sir Thomas Lipton

Royal Sunset

Peace

GAMBLE FRAGRANCE AWARD WINNERS
- Crimson Glory
- Tiffany
- Chrysler Imperial
- Sutter's Gold
- Granada
- Fragrant Cloud
- Papa Meilland
- Sunsprite
- Double Delight
- Fragrant Hour
- Angel Face

The prestigious Gamble Fragrance Award is given to a rose that exhibits a good, strong fragrance but also has good vigor, good pest and disease resistance and good color and is a top seller for more than five years. To date there have been only 11 winners of this award, and these varieties are readily available.

COLOR

Flower color is the feature most people look for when buying and growing roses. Red, pink, yellow, orange, white, mauve, tan and apricot are a few of the colors available, and there is considerable range within each color. For example, pink roses range from light pastel pink to deep pink to vivid neon pink. Flowers can be blends of color including different shades of the same color or two different colors on the same flower—often referred to as a multi-colored flower. Rose petals can be almost every color except black, blue and green. There are roses that look black but are really very deep red. The green-flowered rose, *Rosa chinensis viridiflora,* has no true petals. The green petal-like sepals give the flower its color.

Flower color is affected by sunlight, temperature, soil and water. If your rose has the right environmental conditions and is healthy, you will almost be guaranteed gorgeous blooms.

The International Registration Authority for Roses, run by the ARS, authorizes 18 official colors for all roses. Every new rose variety registered has to list one of the 18 official colors as its color. The color descriptions

Ingrid Bergman

in catalogs and some reference books (including this one) are generally more detailed than the official color listing.

FLOWER FORM

Roses have a variety of flower forms. One of the most familiar is the pointed hybrid tea flower, the classic rose shape we have come to expect when we give or receive roses. Other forms include the flat, single flowers of some species roses and the quartered rosette flowers of some of the old garden roses.

The terms *single, semi-double* and *double* refer to the number of petals and their arrangement on the flower. Single flowers have up to 12 petals arranged in a single row. Semi-double flowers have 13–20 petals arranged in two or three rows. Double flowers have 20 or more petals. Some sources list an additional category for flowers with 35 or more petals. These are called *very double* or *fully double* flowers.

The following are the different rose flower forms:

Flat: Open flowers that are single or semi-double with the petals perpendicular to the stem.

Cupped: Open flowers that are single or semi-double having petals that curve upward forming a shallow cup.

Pointed: Semi-double to double flowers with high-pointed centers created by the tight wrap of petals before they fully unfurl. One of the most familiar forms.

Flat form

Cupped form

Pointed form

Urn-shaped form

Rounded form

Rosette form

Quartered rosette form

Pompom form

Urn-shaped: Semi-double to double flowers with flat tops and slightly outward-curving petals. Similar to the pointed shape but slightly looser and more open in the center.

Rounded: Double flowers with overlapping petals of even size, creating a rounded bowl silhouette.

Rosette: Double flowers with slightly overlapping, unevenly sized petals creating a flattish outline.

Quartered Rosette: Double flowers with petals of uneven size forming a quartered appearance and a flattish outline.

Pompom: Double flowers with many small petals forming a small, rounded outline.

SUBSTANCE

Substance is the amount of moisture in the petals, which affects the texture, firmness, thickness, stability and durability of the petals. Roses have substance at different levels, and rose flowers with substance have a long vase life.

HIPS

Hips are the fruits of roses. They develop when flowers are pollinated, usually by bees. Hips can provide fall and winter interest. They ripen to shades of red, orange and yellow and come in a variety of shapes, from round and globe-like to football shaped to teardrop shaped.

The formation of hips and production of seeds in the hips signal the plant to stop flowering and to prepare for winter dormancy. Not all roses produce hips.

Hips

HARDINESS

The hardiness of a plant is its ability to withstand climatic and other environmental conditions. Cold hardiness designates the plant's ability to survive the minimum average cold temperatures for an area. Some classes of roses, such as the rugosa roses, thrive with no winter protection in areas that get quite cold. Other roses are so tender that they are often grown as annuals and replanted each year. A rose is said to be tender if it cannot survive winter temperatures colder than 10° to 20° F (−12° to −6° C). Hardiness ratings are general, however. Other factors can affect what can and cannot successfully grow in a particular location based on exposure, winds and shelter. These areas are referred to as microclimates.

PLANT FORM

Plant form is the shape and growth habit of the plant. The forms available today can be easily used in the garden and landscape. Growth can be upright, such as the hybrid teas with their straight, sturdy canes. Roses can also have graceful arching canes or can be mounding shrubs that look as good as any of the flowering shrubs used in landscapes. The long, supple canes of climbing and rambling roses can be trained on trellises, fences and

Rose standard

pillars or left to form large, spreading shrubs. Standards, also known as tree roses, have a lollipop look created by budding or grafting a rose plant onto a tall stem. Standards are also available in trailing or spreading forms, resulting in an umbrella-like appearance.

FOLIAGE

Rose foliage can be delicate and fern-like with many leaflets per leaf, such as *Rosa pimpinellifolia*, or large and crinkled as in the rugosa roses. The leaves can be dull or shiny, and colors include dark green, light green or shades of blue-green and gray-green. Some roses have excellent fall color in shades of yellow, red and bronze-red. *Rosa glauca* has beautiful foliar color, bearing blue-green to purple foliage that dramatically contrasts with the pink flowers in season but is most stunning in autumn.

THORNS

What we usually refer to as thorns are really prickles, defined botanically as small, thin, sharp outgrowths of the young bark, whereas thorns are sharp outgrowths from the wood of the stem. Rose prickles come in a variety of sizes and levels of nastiness. The prickles of *Rosa acicularis* (the Prickly Rose) are thin and sharp and cover the stems. The Wingthorn Rose, *Rosa sericea pteracantha*, has large, bright red, winged prickles, which provide color all year. Some roses, such as the Explorer rose Jens Munk, have large, hooked barbs that make pruning a truly dangerous task. Regardless of the type of prickle, handling roses requires care and attention.

Rose foliage can vary in texture and color.

Thorns

Getting Started

Roses are not difficult to grow once you consider a few basics. Planning is essential, though. Good planning will allow you to plant the right rose in the right location for long-term success. Not all roses need the same conditions to perform well. Complete a site analysis, which can be as simple as walking around your garden and observing the conditions at different times of the day or season, to determine if you have the right environment for growing a given rose. You might find it helpful to make an overhead-view scale drawing of your property to plan the layout of your garden.

Climate and Microclimate

Climatic conditions to consider before selecting a rose include the temperature range of your area, the risk and timing of frost, the amount of rainfall, the amount of humidity, prevailing winds and the amount of sunshine available. It is far easier to select a rose that is adapted to your local climate than to battle against the climate. Most roses will grow in a range of hardiness zones, with minimum winter temperature being the most limiting factor. Zones should be used only as guidelines. Some tender roses may be grown in zones colder than they are rated for as long as adequate winter protection is provided. Check the hardiness zones map on page 8 for a general guide to hardiness zones in your area.

A microclimate is an area that has a slightly different climate than the surrounding area. The area to the south side of a building will be warmer than other areas of your yard. The area under the eaves of the house will be drier than other parts of your yard. The top of a hill or slope will be drier than the bottom.

Cold air runs downhill, so the bottom of the slope will be cooler than the top. Part of your site analysis will be to determine the microclimates in your yard. Microclimates enable the gardener to successfully grow roses that are not completely hardy, with minimal to extra winter protection based on the initial zoning.

Nuits de Young

Sun

Roses require a minimum of six hours of sunlight per day for good flowering. Morning sun is best as it helps the foliage dry quickly, lessening the chance of fungal disease. Any

Tabris

Golden Beryl

rose grown in full shade will be weak and spindly with very few to no flowers. Some roses are better adapted to growing in light to partial shade. (See the list of shade-tolerant roses on p. 92.) If your garden gets intensely hot in summer, some light afternoon shade will help prevent sun damage to the flowers and foliage.

Wind

Wind can be the enemy of roses, increasing evaporation from the soil and drying a rose out quickly, especially when there has been little rain. A strong wind can dry and shred flowers. Winter wind can dry and destroy flower buds and canes. Protect your roses from the prevailing winds with fences, buildings and hedges.

Some wind, however, can help roses. A gentle breeze helps keep foliage dry, minimizing the incidence of disease. That breeze can also carry the fragrance of a rose a long way.

Competition

Roses are heavy feeders and drinkers. They expend a great deal of energy producing their flowers and don't like to share root space with many other plants. Trees, turf, weeds and other garden plants may compete with roses for space and resources. In particular, avoid planting roses near trees such as spruce, ash, poplar and elm, which have large, wide-spreading root systems. Plants with shallow, well-behaved root systems are good companions for roses.

Soil

Soil provides support for the plant, holds and provides nutrients and water and makes oxygen available to the roots. Roses prefer a fertile, well-drained, moisture-holding loam with at least five percent organic matter, but they can grow in a wide range of soil types.

Testing a location's drainage

Soil is made up of particles of different sizes. Clay particles are very small or fine, silt particles are slightly larger but still considered fine, and sand particles are the largest of the three. Soils with a high percentage of clay particles are considered heavy, while soils with a high percentage of sand particles are considered light. Heavy soils hold water and nutrients but their drainage is very poor. Loams are soils with a balanced mix of clay, silt and sand particles. Roses like loams and clay-based soils as long as there is adequate drainage. Sandy soils require more frequent watering and fertilizing.

It is important to consider the pH level (the scale on which acidity or alkalinity is measured) of soil, which influences the availability of nutrients. An acid soil has a pH under 7.0 while an alkaline soil has a pH over 7.0. Roses perform best in slightly acidic soils, with pH between 6.0 and 7.0. Soil pH can be changed but it takes a long time and routine applications of either sulfur or lime to maintain the desired level. It is a good idea to check the pH of your soil at least every two years.

SOIL TESTING

Complete soil testing kits are available from private or government labs. A complete soil test will tell you the pH; the percentage of sand, silt, clay and organic matter; the amount and type of nutrients available and the degree of salinity. This information helps you plan your fertilizing program, and laboratories often provide recommendations for correcting soil deficiencies. (See Soil Testing in Resources, p. 264.)

Garden centers sell simple test kits for pH and some major nutrients. Based on the results of the test, the garden center staff should be able to make some recommendations about which amendments to use and how to use them. Soil amendments are used to improve fertility, drainage and workability. Read about amendments in the Planting Roses section of this introduction.

It may also be a good idea to have your water tested, especially if you are using well water. Knowing the pH, mineral composition and salt content of your water source can help identify problems. Some nutrients can be rendered unavailable to plants depending on the mineral content of your water.

DRAINAGE

Roses use a lot of water but do not like to have their roots sitting in water. The soil must drain well enough to allow air to reach the roots and hold enough water for the rose to use. Heavy soils can have the drainage improved by adding organic matter or gypsum, by installing perforated drainage tile under the roses or by double digging the soil (see p. 34). Sandy soils drain water quickly but do not retain nutrients for long. Organic matter helps sandy soils hold more water and nutrients.

If you are unsure that the spot you have chosen will drain well enough to prevent standing water, try this simple test. Dig a test hole that is 12" (30 cm) wide and deep. Fill the hole to the top with water and let it drain completely. Fill the hole with water again and note the time it takes for the water to completely drain from the hole. A drainage rate of $1/2$" (1.3 cm) or less per hour is considered poor and will limit plant selection or require expensive drainage work to alleviate the problem.

Escapade

Buying Roses

Roses can be purchased from nurseries, garden centers, mail-order suppliers, supermarkets and department stores. You will likely get the best plants and advice from nurseries, garden centers and mail-order suppliers that specialize in roses. Roses that are produced locally are good choices because they are already adapted to the climate. Ordering roses through the mail or over the internet is very convenient and the roses come right to your door (see Resources, p. 262).

Roses are available for sale in three ways: bare-root, packaged bare-root and containerized (in pots).

Some roses come bare-root, especially from mail-order nurseries. These roses are dug up from the field when they are dormant. The soil is removed from the roots and the roots are wrapped in plastic, newspaper or wood wool before shipping. Ideally the roses should arrive in the dormant state with no new growth.

The roses sometimes start growing during transport. Before planting, remove shoots longer than 2" (5 cm).

Packaged bare-root roses are often found in supermarkets and department stores. Each rose comes in a plastic or waxed cardboard container with the roots surrounded by moist sawdust, peat moss, wood chips or shredded paper. Buy packaged roses early in the season when the roses are still relatively dormant. Even if you

Bare-root roses are generally less expensive than container roses. Container roses are more common and convenient.

can't plant them right away, you can store them in a cool location. The canes of packaged roses are usually waxed to prevent the canes from drying out during shipping and before planting. The wax will come off during the growing season. Roses with waxed canes are better choices than roses with unwaxed canes.

Container roses are grown in pots, not fields, though some stock sold in containers may have been bare-root plants potted by the nursery staff. Own-root roses (see below) are commonly available as container stock. Container roses are available throughout the growing season and can be planted any time. Often a container rose will be in flower and you can see exactly what you are purchasing.

Grafted Plants

Most roses available today are bud-grafted, a process in which a bud eye from a selected variety is grafted onto the rootstock of another variety. When the bud starts to grow, the top of the rootstock plant is removed. The energy that would have been used by the top is all directed towards the newly grafted bud. The area where the new bud is grafted onto the rootstock is called the bud union.

Budded plants mature more quickly than plants from cuttings. Some growers claim the flowers from

a grafted plant are bigger and better than flowers from the same variety grown on its own roots. At one time it was believed that using a cold-hardy rootstock would increase the cold hardiness of the grafted variety, but in fact only the rootstock remains hardy and its hardiness does not transfer to the variety grafted on top of it.

Growers and hybridizers have many rootstocks available and choose a rootstock that will provide the desired characteristics. Always ask the supplier if the rootstock is appropriate for your area. For our area *Rosa multiflora* is the best rootstock. Be cautious when ordering roses from the United States, as they may be grafted onto Dr. Huey rootstock, which is not well-suited, in the long term, to our area.

Standard roses, often referred to as tree roses, have two grafts and an elongated main stem. The lower graft is between the rootstock and the stem. The other graft is between the stem and the variety at the top. Standard roses do not fit into any specific rose class, because the variety grafted to the top could be a miniature, floribunda or hybrid tea.

Own-root Plants

Own-root plants, as the name suggests, are grown on their own roots. They take longer to reach maturity than bud-grafted plants and are more expensive to produce but can be very long-lived and are hardier than grafted plants. Not having a bud union allows for a more natural plant form as the top growth does not all originate from one point. It also eliminates a weak point (the bud union) that is susceptible to attack by pests or damage from cold weather. Old garden roses, miniature roses, species roses, ramblers and climbers are often grown on their own roots. Own-root roses are inclined to spread by suckers from the roots. They might end up everywhere in your garden.

What to Look For

When buying a rose, make sure the roots are moist. It is easy to check for moist soil if the rose is in a container. It is more difficult, but possible, to examine the roots of packaged roses. If the package is very light or you can see any dry soil or planting mix, the roots are probably dry.

Examine the root system. Bare-root roses should have a mass of long, fibrous roots. Avoid roses that have short spindly roots or that have had their roots pruned. Ensure that the roots of container roses have white tips and are not encircling the inside of the container or growing out the bottom of the container. Avoid plants with blackened or girdled roots. Roses with a weak root system will have a tough time establishing.

The canes of bare-root and packaged roses should be supple and dark green, have small buds and be at least as thick as a pencil no matter the grade (see sidebar). Avoid plants with dry, shriveled canes. Any visible pith should be white or green. Roses with tan or brown piths may have sustained some damage.

On grafted roses examine the rootstock neck just below the bud union. It should be at least as big around as your thumb with no visible external damage. The neck should be no longer than about 3" (8 cm), because if it is any longer planting could be awkward. Avoid bare-root roses with long, pale shoots.

Roses are sorted into three grades according to the size and number of main canes. More often than not, you'll come across only Grade 1 or Grade 1½ roses, indicating that the rose you've chosen is of excellent quality. It is best to invest a little more money when purchasing a rose, ensuring that it is of superior quality. Don't settle for cheap roses—the old cliché rings true: you get what you pay for.

Root-bound plant

Planting Roses

Preparing the proper planting site is an investment of time that will be rewarded when your rose blooms well. Proper care, placement and planting are critical to a rose's establishment and long-term success. Preparing the soil is the most important step, and it can begin long before planting.

Preparing the Soil

Based on a soil test (see p. 29 and Soil Testing, p. 264), amend your soil as necessary with organic or inorganic amendments. Especially if you are planting a large area of roses, you should prepare the area the summer prior to spring planting so the soil has a chance to settle over winter before you plant your roses. If the soil settles too much, it is easy to top it up before planting. You can prepare the soil just before planting, but be aware that your rose might settle more deeply than is recommended.

There are many possible methods for preparing an area to plant roses. The following method is referred to as double digging and is a little easier than some of the others. Dig and set aside the topsoil from the planting area. Turn over the subsoil with a

Topsoil set aside

Adding amendments to subsoil

Mixing soil and amendments

Adding amendments to topsoil

garden fork. To accommodate bush roses such as hybrid teas, grandifloras and floribundas, the prepared area should be 18–24" (46–61 cm) deep and 24" (61 cm) wide for each rose. If you are planting miniatures then the depth and width can be 12" (30 cm). Robust climbers, ramblers and shrub roses may need an area up to 18–24" (46–61 cm) deep and 4' (1.2 m) wide.

Sometimes it is impossible to dig the soil to the desired depth because of rock or hardpan. You can use a raised bed to provide the necessary soil depth and drainage, you can try to break through the hardpan or you can choose a different location.

Add any amendments and mix them in well, then replace the topsoil. If possible, the area should sit for a few months to settle.

Organic soil amendments include compost, well-rotted manure (preferably cow or sheep manure), peat moss, leaf mold, bonemeal, alfalfa pellets and agricultural byproducts such as seed shells and husks, sawdust and composted wood chips. Inorganic amendments include gypsum (calcium sulfate), superphosphate, limestone, coarse sand, vermiculite and perlite. Each amendment has different properties and should be added to the soil only if deemed necessary, on the basis of a soil test.

Use only thoroughly composted materials. Amendments such as fresh manure may burn a rose's roots, and uncomposted organic materials, such as sawdust or woodchips, use

If you are considering using mushroom compost, check with the supplier to ensure the compost has low salt and is pesticide free.

the available nitrogen from the soil to aid their decomposition.

A common practice for rose growers is to add 25–33% of soil volume of compost or well-rotted manure— for example, adding 3–4" (7.6–10 cm) of compost or well-rotted manure to soil at a depth of 12" (30 cm).

When to Plant

Roses establish best in cool, moist soil. Planting in spring is best, from March to early May. Bare-root roses are planted in spring while they're still dormant. They can be planted in fall in warmer regions of the Pacific Northwest but only if the plants become available at that time of year. They should be planted immediately after purchase so they may become established before the ground freezes. Fall planting of bare-root roses is not recommended in colder regions of the Pacific Northwest.

Container roses can be planted in spring, summer or fall. Container roses are the only roses that can be planted in summer because they already have an established root system. Diligent watering is mandatory for proper establishment of container roses and even moreso for

Soaking bare-root roses

If you buy a container rose, the preparation begins at the point of purchase. Make sure that the rose is thoroughly saturated before taking it home to ensure that the roots remain moist during transport. If you are transporting the rose home in a car, be aware of the temperature, as excess heat quickly dries plants out. If you are using an open truck for transport, lay the plant down or cover it to protect it from the wind, as even a short trip can be traumatic for a plant.

those planted in summer. If planting in fall, plant no later than mid-November and at least three to four weeks before the ground is expected to freeze.

Preparing the Rose

All roses should be planted as soon as possible after purchase. Your new rose will require some preparation.

If you are going to plant within 24 hours, stand the roses in a bucket of muddy water, ensuring the roots are completely covered with water. Some rosarians soak the entire plant. The mud in the water will lightly coat the roots, helping to prevent desiccation during planting. Soak the plant for 12 to 24 hours but no longer.

If you have to store the roses for a couple of days, do not remove the packaging but open it just enough to

Heeling-in bare-root roses

check that the roots are moist, adding water if necessary. Close the package and place it in a cool, dry, frost-free area such as a refrigerator or an unheated garage.

If your garden is still frozen or too muddy to work when your packaged or bare-root roses arrive, you will need longer storage. The usual method is called heeling-in, which involves digging a trench in a well-drained area such as an edge of a vegetable garden or under an eave, preferably with shade. The trench should be 12" (30 cm) deep on one side with the bottom of the trench sloping up at a 45-degree angle. Lay the roses in the trench with the roots towards the bottom of the trench. Cover completely with soil except for the tips of the canes, and water the entire trench well. Keeping the tips uncovered helps you find the rose later, and the soil covering keeps the roses from drying out.

Dainty Bess

This method is great as long as the weather remains somewhat cool. If freezing weather is in the forecast, cover the heeled-in roses with mulch or burlap. Some sources say that heeled-in roses can be stored for a few months, but it is best to plant as soon as possible. Use caution when digging up heeled-in roses to avoid damage to the roots and canes. Long-term storage is usually not necessary as mail-order suppliers time their shipments to coincide with the arrival of spring in your area.

Container roses will likely have to be hardened off before planting. Hardening off is the process of slowly acclimatizing a plant to its new surroundings. Sometimes this is done at the nursery; sometimes container roses have just come out of the greenhouse. When purchasing the rose, ask whether it's been hardened off and when it is safe to plant. If is still requires hardening off, begin by giving the plant a little sun each day and protecting it from stiff wind and freezing at night. Gradually increase the amount of time the rose is in the sunlight, wind and evening cold. The process should take about a week.

Preparing the Hole

In your prepared rose area, you must dig a hole for each rose. The ideal situation is to have the holes dug in the prepared area before your roses arrive. Doing so is sometimes impossible, however, because you may not know what kind of rose you're buying.

For container stock, the depth in the center of the hole should be equal to the depth of the rootball, and one-and-a-half times the width of the container. Certain classes of roses may need to be planted deeper than others. Roses that are not as hardy need to be planted deeper, especially if there is a bud union that needs protection.

For bare-root stock, the hole is usually 24" (61 cm) deep and wide, big enough to completely contain the expanded roots with a little extra room on the sides and a cone-shaped central mound (see diagram). The mound helps to evenly space the roots in the hole, prevents the rose from sinking as the soil settles and encourages excess water to drain away from the roots. Some rose growers form the mound in the center of the hole with amended backfill rather than soil alone.

It is a good idea to roughen the sides of the hole with a garden fork or trowel so that it's easier for roots to penetrate out of the hole.

Placing the Rose

Plant your rose on an overcast or rainy day. If this is not possible, try to plant it during the early morning or early evening, when the temperatures are lower, rather than in the middle of the day.

BARE-ROOT ROSES

Remove the plastic and sawdust from the roots or retrieve the rose from your temporary storage. Prune out any broken, diseased or rotten roots or canes. Center the plant over

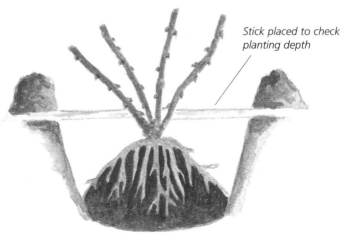

Stick placed to check planting depth

Bare-root stock on central mound

the central mound and fan out the roots in the hole.

If your rose is grafted, the depth of the bud union is important. Plant the union approximately 2" (5 cm) below the surface of the soil. In colder areas, plant it at a depth of 3–4" (8–10 cm). Some growers recommend that for tender grafted roses the bud union be planted at a depth of 6" (15 cm) in zone 3 or colder. Basically, the colder the zone, the deeper the bud union. If the rootstock neck is excessively long—3" (8 cm) or more—plant the rose at an angle, so the roots are not too deep but the bud union is at the correct depth.

Cut the remaining canes of hybrid teas, grandifloras and floribundas to a height of 10–12" (25–30 cm). Some rosarians cut the canes to 5–8" (13–20 cm), which causes the new canes to form lower on the plant, giving a much bushier look. Recent research has shown that roses perform better with more foliage. Allowing weaker canes to grow will provide the rose with more foliage and thus more energy in its establishment year. Other than to remove broken or diseased canes, fall-planted container roses should not be cut back until all other roses are cut back for winter.

CONTAINER ROSES

Container roses are very easy to plant. Containers are made of plastic or pressed fiber. Before planting, water the rootball thoroughly and gently remove the container to check the root mass. If the plant is girdled or root-bound (if the roots circle around the inside of the container between the container and the soil), the roots must be loosened. Any large roots encircling the soil or growing into the center of the root mass instead of outward should be removed before planting. A sharp pair of hand pruners (secateurs) or a pocket knife will work very well for

Central mound

Planting a container rose

Checking planting depth

this task. Some roses might not have been in their containers long enough to develop enough roots to allow the container to be removed without soil falling away. If soil falls away from the roots, the new feeder roots can be damaged, but do not be discouraged. Treat the rose as bare-root stock for planting.

All containers must be removed before planting. Although some containers appear to be made of peat moss or natural fibers, they won't be able to decompose as fast as growing roots require. The roots may not be able to penetrate the pot sides, and the fiber will wick moisture away from the roots. The roots may never

When planting container grafted roses, make sure that the bud union is the same depth as that required by bare-root roses.

even leave the pot, resulting in girdled, constricted roots.

Place the rose, pot and all, on top of the central mound to check planting depth, adjusting if necessary. Remove the pot and place the rootball onto the central mound. Prune out any dead or diseased canes.

MINIATURES

Most miniature roses are sold as container roses and can be planted the same way as larger container roses. Most miniatures are grown in greenhouses and must be hardened off before planting.

STANDARD ROSES

Standard roses usually have two bud unions. When planting standard roses, ensure the lower bud union is at the proper depth. Use a sturdy, rot-proof stake long enough to be set into undisturbed soil and reach up to just below the top bud union. The stake can be placed on the sunny side, which helps protect the main

Backfilling hole

50% backfilled

Adding fertilizer to backfill

Settling backfill with water

Settling backfilled topsoil with water

Planting process complete

stem from sun scald, or to the side of the prevailing wind for extra support. Tie the main stem to the stake about halfway up the stake and near the top. Prune the top as for bare-root plantings.

ROOT PRUNING

We do not recommend root pruning when planting or transplanting, other than removing broken, diseased or dead roots for bare-root plantings. Scientific studies have confirmed that root pruning physiologically shocks the plant by throwing hormones out of balance. It increases water and nutrient stresses as well as the susceptibility of the rose to insect and disease attacks.

Backfill

With the rose in the hole it is time to replace the soil. Container stock will usually stay upright during backfilling while a bare-root rose will need to be held in position.

If you have not already amended the soil in your rose bed, amend the backfill soil. Leaf mold, well-rotted manure, compost, bonemeal and moist peat moss are all suitable amendments.

When backfilling, it is important to have good root-to-soil contact to help the plant's stability and establishment. Large air pockets remaining after backfilling could cause unwanted settling and increase the risk of desiccation. Tamping or stepping down on the backfilled soil used to be recommended, but the risk of injuring the roots and compacting the soil has made this practice fall out of favor. Use water to settle the soil gently around the roots and in the hole, taking care not to drown the plant. Backfill in small amounts bit by bit rather than all at once. Add some soil then water it in, repeating until the hole is full.

Use any soil remaining after backfilling to top up the soil level around

treewell

Protecting newly planted rose with mounded soil

the plant after the backfilled soil settles and to mound up around the canes. Some rose gardeners add perlite or coarse sand to the area immediately around the bud union to make it easier for shoots arising from the bud union to break through to the surface.

Amending the backfill in heavy clay soils will provide a light soil medium for the root system to grow in until the roots reach the heavy clay. Some of the roots will have difficulty penetrating through the clay, resulting in what is known as 'flower pot syndrome,' when the roots grow only in and around the amended soil, as if the rose was actually grown in a clay flowerpot. You could take the time to amend heavy subsoil by removing it and amending it before backfilling. If you don't want to amend so extensively, it will help to at least score the bottom of the planting hole with a garden fork to help the roots break through the heavy soil.

Bonemeal is a slow-release fertilizer and will gradually add important nutrients for root development. When integrating bonemeal into the backfill, be wary of moles, which like bonemeal and will dig around the soil to find it, damaging the roots.

Planting tip
Steep willow twigs in water for a week and use the water when settling the backfill soil and when first watering the newly planted rose. The water contains a natural rooting hormone and salicylic acid, which both aid in root regeneration.

Protecting the Rose
Once the rose is in the hole and properly backfilled, mound soil over it to a depth of 10–12" (25–30 cm), less if the canes are shorter. If you do not have enough soil, you can use mulch. Mounding the soil helps prevent desiccation of the canes while the rose rebuilds its feeder roots. Ensure the entire mound is moist and remains moist.

In three to four weeks, less if the weather is good, the bud eyes will swell and produce new canes and foliage. When you can see the new growth, slowly remove the mound. Choose overcast or rainy days for this task. Hot sunny days will scorch the newly exposed, delicate shoots. It should take about a week to remove the mound, enough time to allow the new, tender growth a chance to harden off. If there is a risk of frost, recover the rose with soil or mulch.

If the rose fails to break dormancy, mound with moist peat and cover with plastic, creating a mini greenhouse. Check daily to ensure the humidity under the plastic is not causing disease or rot to form and the peat remains moist but not soggy. Allow new growth to harden off as stated above. If the rose still does not break dormancy, cut the canes and look at the pith. If the pith is brown and there are no white tips

Staggered double-row hedge

on the roots, it's time to dig up the rose and get a replacement.

Transplanting

Roses are said to dislike being moved once established, but the need may arise. The younger the rose, the more likely it will be able to re-establish successfully when moved to a new location.

If you are moving a rose to a spot where another rose previously grew, add fresh soil or lots of compost, as the previous rose may have depleted the soil of nutrients. It is equally important to use fresh soil or lots of compost when planting a new rose in a spot where a diseased rose was removed. There may be populations of organisms in the old soil that could use the rose as a host plant, such as soil fungi, viruses and nematodes. This is sometimes referred to as **soil sickness**. The bad organisms attack the young feeder roots of new roses, limiting the rose's ability to absorb water and nutrients. Planting your rose with fresh soil will provide a new source of nutrients and aid in its establishment.

Transplanting roses can be complicated. A local rose growers' society should be able to provide detailed information or direct you to it.

Planting Methods for Different Landscape Uses

Roses can be used for a variety of landscape uses. There are some things to keep in mind when planting for specific landscape situations.

HEDGES

When planting hedges, staggering the rows allows the maximum number of roses for the size of the hedge, gives a good mass effect and allows all the roses to be seen from one side. Modern bush roses are often staggered, with 18–24" (46–61 cm) between plants. The more vigorous shrub roses are planted at two-thirds of the spread at maturity so the branches eventually intermingle to form the hedge. For taller hedges, planting distance can be increased slightly. The best rose hedges are grown from own-root roses because any suckers developing from the roots will help thicken up the hedge and are from the rose variety you planted.

Some rosarians suggest that soil sickness does not exist. Regardless, adding fresh soil and amendments when replacing a diseased rose with a new one can only be a benefit.

CLIMBERS

Planting climbers requires some extra preparation. Have the support structure in place and a supply of rose ties. Special rose ties are available at your local garden center or from specialty rose nurseries, but rose ties can be any piece of non-abrasive material used to tie the rose to the supports. Support can consist of stiff wires strung horizontally along a wall or hooks attached to a wooden fence. Hooks make rose maintenance and training a little easier, as the canes merely have to be set into the hooks rather than tied to a wire. It really doesn't matter what the support is as long as it is sturdy enough to support the weight of the plant in full bloom.

Plant the rose about 18" (46 cm) from the wall, fence or whatever you have chosen to train the climber on. Angle the canes toward the lowest support and tie in place. You will want the canes to form a fan shape as you attach them to the support.

Leave enough room between the tie and the structure for the cane to grow—your finger should fit easily into the space. This will prevent the growing cane from being strangled.

Single-row hedge

GROUNDCOVERS

When planting roses as a groundcover, you must first remove any weeds. An easy, non-toxic method is to pasteurize the soil:

- Remove any surface weeds
- Rake the area smooth and cover it with a sheet of flexible black plastic
- Bury the edges of the plastic and leave in place for a couple of months. The heat under the plastic will prevent annual weed seeds, soil diseases and insects from penetrating into the soil
- Remove the plastic
- Plant, disturbing the soil as little as possible.

The way you space and plant groundcover roses will depend on what roses you are using. A rule of thumb is to space at two-thirds of the spread at maturity. For consistency and a good massing effect, all the roses should be the same variety. After planting the roses, cover the entire area with mulch, being careful not to mound the mulch directly around the crown of the rose.

PLANTING IN CONTAINERS

Planting roses in containers is different from planting container roses which are often meant to be put in their pots temporarily. Any rose can be planted in a container, but be aware that the larger the rose, the larger the container you will need and the heavier it will be once it is filled with soil. If the containers are too heavy to lift, casters on the bottom of the container can be used for ease

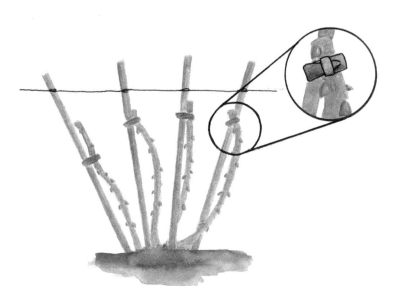

Attaching climber or rambler canes to support

of movement. Containers can be made of many different materials such as wood, plastic, metal or clay. Straight-sided containers offer more room for the roots than those with tapered sides. Ensure the bottom of the container has an adequate number of drainage holes. Choose a container that won't be so heavy that it's difficult to move, especially when full of moist dirt. There are pots made of materials such as fiberglass and plastic resins that look like terracotta or ceramic but are light and last much longer than natural materials.

Smaller containers will require water and fertilizer more often. Choose a container that will accommodate the rootball's growth over a long period of time.

Pink Petticoat

Roses grown on their own roots (old garden roses or species roses) do not have a bud union. The crown should be planted 1" (2.5 cm) below soil level or at the same level it is in the pot.

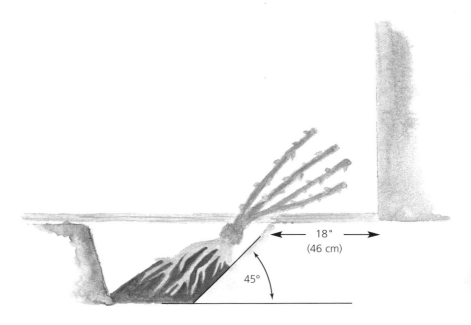

18"
(46 cm)

45°

Proper planting distance and angle for climbers and ramblers

Lavaglow

Beauty Secret

Floribundas, polyanthas, miniatures and the smaller hybrid teas are excellent choices for containers. Miniatures can be in containers as small as 12" (30 cm) in diameter and 10–12" (25–30 cm) deep. Floribundas, polyanthas and hybrid teas should have pots with a minimum 16" (41 cm) diameter and depth. For standard roses, match the container size to what is needed by the variety grafted to the top of the standard.

The soil for containers must be non-compacting, moderately rich, moisture holding and well drained. Sterile planting mixes, some specifically designed for roses, are available from your local nursery or garden center. Sterile mixes won't provide any nutrients to the rose, however, so make sure to supplement with a regular fertilizing program. A good mix is one-third loam, one-third organic matter such as compost or well-rotted manure and one-third coarse sand. When ordering soil, specify loam and not topsoil, and to ensure good results, test the pH of any soil you bring in to your rose garden. When planted and settled, the soil should be 1–2" (2.5–5 cm) below the rim of the container to facilitate a thorough watering without run-off.

Planting in a container is similar to planting in the ground. Place the rose in the container and backfill in the same way as if you were planting in the ground.

Plants in containers may need protection from extreme temperatures. Rot-resistant wood such as cedar makes an attractive container that offers protection from excessive heating and cooling. Containers made of other materials may need help keeping the roots cool. One method is to place one container into another with at least 1" (2.5 cm) between the containers for insulating material such as moistened vermiculite, sawdust or Styrofoam packing peanuts. Alternatively, the inside of a container may be lined with stiff foam insulation for straight-sided containers or a couple of layers of carpet underlay for curved-side containers.

Ingrid Bergman

Don't use gravel at the bottom of your container. Studies have shown that the soil on top of the gravel must be completely saturated with water before it drains through the gravel beneath. A fiberglass or metal window screen is better for covering the drainage holes on the bottom of the container; water will drain out but soil will not.

Green Ice

Caring for Roses

Watering

Watering is probably the most important maintenance practice for roses. Roses, especially repeat-blooming roses, need moisture for good blooming. If your soil has good drainage, it is difficult to overwater. However, overwatering and overfeeding creates large flowers and lush growth, which are susceptible to attacks by insects and disease. The soil, wind, amount of sunlight, daylight temperature and amount of rainfall all must be considered when determining how much water to apply and when to apply it. Sandy soil will require more frequent watering than clay soil. Sandy soil takes less time to get water to the correct depth than clay soil. Roses in windy locations will need more water than roses in sheltered locations. If the sun is particularly hot, the rose will need extra water.

A rain gauge indicates how much rain has fallen, but be aware that rainfall may not supply all a rose's water needs. Check your roses daily throughout the growing season. If the soil is dry several inches below the soil surface, it needs water. If you notice the leaves wilting, water immediately.

Container roses should be watered daily—water until the water comes out the holes in the bottom of the container—though larger containers generally need water less often than smaller containers. Do not use a saucer or tray underneath any outdoor container. During rains the saucer will trap water which can drown the roots.

A general guideline is to apply 1" (2.5 cm) of water per week or about 5 gallons (25 liters) per plant. You

Purple Pavement

will have to determine what watering regime is right for your area and soil composition. When you apply water, it should penetrate through the rootzone to a depth of at least 18" (46 cm). Shallow watering promotes root growth near the surface rather than deep root growth. Shallow roots may be damaged by cultivation or weeding, may suffer fertilizer burn and are susceptible to drought conditions.

To determine if you are watering deeply enough, dig a small hole beside the rose and see how far down the water has penetrated. For example, if you water for 15 minutes and the water has gone down 9" (23 cm), you know you need to water for a total of 30 minutes to get water to a depth of 18" (46 cm). Give the water at least half an hour or so to soak in before you check how far it has penetrated. Another method of measuring soil penetration is poking a stick into the watered soil. If the stick moves easily through the soil, the soil is wet enough; if the stick does not move easily, the soil is too dry. You can also use a soil probe. Soil probes are hollow tubes with a T-handle with the lower part of the hollow tube cut away on one side. They are available at irrigation supply businesses and some garden centers.

Watering in spring begins when the ground has almost completely thawed. Your rose will not need as much water at the beginning of spring as it does in mid-summer but you still must water deeply. In spring ensure you water any dry beds and

Belle Amour

Rosa glauca

any roses under house eaves. Ease back on watering in fall to help the rose prepare itself for winter.

There are different ways to water. Using a hose and watering wand with a flood nozzle allows you to observe each rose close up. It is a great method but time consuming. Using sprinklers takes less of your attention but the amount of water making it to the plant's rootzone is affected by wind and evaporation. If you are using a sprinkler, it is best to water in the morning to give the foliage a chance to dry in the morning sun. Wet foliage is an invitation to fungal diseases. Watering in the morning also reduces the amount of evaporation that can occur when watering in the hot afternoon sun. Soaker hoses are widely available. They are easy to use and apply water directly to the rootzone without wetting the foliage.

Efficient watering techniques are especially important in areas with imposed water restrictions during hot and dry summers. You can reduce the amount of watering you need to do by adding mulch, by using drought-tolerant roses such as rugosa, China, species or Explorer series roses or by creating a treewell.

A treewell is a low mound of soil 2–6" (5–15 cm) high built up in a ring around the outer edge of the planting hole. Treewells contain the water underneath the plant, not allowing the water to flow away before soaking in. When watering roses with treewells, fill the treewell to the top and leave it. Water your other roses and plants, then come back and fill the reservoir again. You might have to fill the treewell four to five times depending on the volume of the treewell. The treewell will be most useful during dry periods and should be removed during rainy periods to prevent the roots from becoming waterlogged.

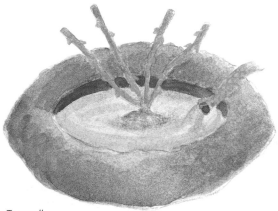

Treewell

Mulching

Mulching is placing a layer of organic or inorganic material on top of the soil around the base of the rose. Mulching slows evaporation, keeps roots cool, protects roots from damage from cultivation, suppresses weed growth and prevents soil-borne diseases from splashing onto the foliage. Mulching allows feeder roots to grow near the surface, increasing the rose's ability to absorb nutrients and water. Mulching prevents soil from crusting over or becoming compacted. Organic mulch also improves the soil as soil organisms decompose it, releasing nutrients and maintaining an open structure that encourages root penetration. Mulching looks good, giving the bed a finished, natural appearance.

A Morden Fireglow plant with mulch

Organic mulches include compost, well-rotted manure (fresh manure can burn roots), pine and spruce needles, shredded leaves, shredded bark, grass clippings and locally available agricultural byproducts. Inorganic mulches include gravel, rocks, plastic and landscape fabric. Inorganic mulches can make winterizing and spring cleanup very difficult. We recommend organic mulches for the benefit they provide to the soil.

Morden Ruby

If you choose to use grass clippings as mulch, ensure the grass was not treated with herbicide that can harm the rose. Do not add grass clippings after the end of August, as the grass could add nitrogen to the soil, stimulating growth that will likely suffer winter kill. Avoid using peat

If you live in a big city, your roses may get covered in dust and pollutants, which inhibit photosynthesis. Wash roses once a week, in the morning so the foliage dries quickly. Washing roses also helps keep the spider mite and aphid populations down to a minimum.

moss alone as a mulch. It is very light and can blow away in the wind. Alone it dries quickly, and when dry it repels moisture. Mixed with other materials, peat moss is a suitable organic mulch.

Mulch may rob some nitrogen from the soil as it decomposes throughout the season. Compensate by applying a small amount of nitrogen fertilizer, such as fish fertilizer, when laying the mulch. Avoid sawdust, especially from pressure-treated lumber and softwood trees, as it may release oils that retard plant growth. Other materials to avoid are walnut leaves, large leaves and redwood mulch. Walnut leaves and redwood mulch are toxic to rose growth when they break down. Large leaves tend to mat together, restricting air and water movement. Shred and compost large leaves

Cardinal de Richelieu

before using as mulch. Shredded bark mulches are better and more aesthetically pleasing than large chunks or nuggets.

A good mulch allows air and water to penetrate into the soil. Apply mulch to a depth of 3" (8 cm), thick enough to suppress weeds and still allow air circulation into the soil. Keep the mulch 1–2" (2.5–5 cm) away from the base of the rose.

Fertilizing

The best start for roses is to dig well-rotted manure or compost and any organic amendments prescribed by the soil test into the soil during preparation (see Preparing the Soil, p. 34). Even if you have amended the soil for your roses before planting, you still need an ongoing program of fertilizing throughout the growing season.

Fertilizing roses is complex but not necessarily difficult. The fertility program for your roses depends on the type of roses you are growing and the nutrients available in your soil. Modern roses, such as hybrid teas and grandifloras, are heavy feeders that grow best in a rich, fertile soil. If you are growing species roses to naturalize an area, you will not fertilize to the same extent. If in doubt about fertilizing, contact a rose society in your area, which can provide information or put you in touch with someone who can help you develop a fertilizing program. A soil test will dictate what the soil needs. Don't add fertilizer just for the sake of adding it. You may end up feeding your roses to death; too much fertilizer will not benefit your rose, only damage it.

The key to a successful fertility program is to feed the soil, not the plant. Healthy soils are dynamic ecosystems containing thousands of soil organisms that work in harmony with each other and the plants growing in them. Any practice that disrupts the balance of the soil ecosystem can mean problems for plants. Perhaps the chemical fertilizer you are using has changed the pH of the soil, making it difficult for the soil microorganisms to thrive. They can no longer break down the organic matter in the soil to provide the plant with nutrients, leaving your plant dependent on chemicals for nutrients. When the soil is out of ecological balance, insects and diseases can move in. If you take care of your soil, it will produce good quality roses.

A healthy City of York

WHEN TO FERTILIZE

The first fertilization of the year is just after spring pruning or when winter protection is completely removed. The last fertilization of the year should be four to six weeks before the first frost. Frost can damage late, lush growth, so you don't want to fertilize too close to first frost. A safe approach is to stop using nitrogen fertilizers in mid-summer and fertilize after that time with fall fertilizer, which is high in potassium.

Species roses, shrub roses and other once-flowering roses can be fertilized once a year in spring. The minimum fertilization for repeat bloomers is once in spring and once when the first flush of blooms is finished. Newly planted roses should be fertilized lightly six weeks after planting.

WHAT TO USE

The numbers on a package of chemical fertilizer, for example 24–14–14 or 20–24–14, represent nitrogen, phosphorous and potassium, respectively. The numbers are referred to as the 'fertilizer analysis.' The higher the number, the greater the amount of nutrient. A fertilizer with all three nutrients is called a complete fertilizer. Fertilizers that are

Hansa

Love

specifically designed for roses contain the nutrients most needed by roses. Follow the directions on the package for proper application rates, methods and precautions.

Organic and chemical fertilizers are available in granular and liquid forms. Granular fertilizers are small, dry particles that can be easily spread by machine or hand. Granular chemical fertilizers have nitrogen available in either quick-release or slow-release formulations. Quick-release fertilizers provide a big shot of plant-available nitrogen in a short time. Too much nitrogen too quickly will favor foliage growth over flowers. It may burn the roots and the foliage. It may also create lush growth that is susceptible to insects and diseases. Slow-release fertilizers are a better choice because they release their nutrients over a long period, lowering the potential for burning, excessive vegetative growth and leaching of the fertilizer into the groundwater. Granular organic fertilizers are naturally slow releasing. Many rosarians will supplement their slow-release fertility program with a small amount of quick-release nitrogen to ensure the rose is adequately fed.

Liquid fertilizers come as liquid concentrate or powder that is mixed with water and applied to the soil or sprayed on the leaves. The most common soil-applied liquid fertilizer formulation is 20–20–20, but there are organic options available.

Organic fertilizers include well-rotted manure, fish emulsion, fish meal, bloodmeal (high in nitrogen), alfalfa pellets, compost, bonemeal, wood ashes and seaweed extracts. A good, balanced organic fertilizer mix for roses is three parts alfalfa meal, one part bonemeal and one part wood ash. Compost tea (see recipe) can be used as a liquid feed.

Organic fertilizers are better for the health of the soil. For example, seaweed extracts such as kelp not only supply micronutrients, they also contain a substance that releases micronutrients already in the soil. (Micronutrients are organic compounds essential in minute amounts to the health of the plant.) When applied as a foliar feed in spring and fall, the seaweed extracts also help improve roses' cold hardiness and drought resistance. Fish emulsion and fish meal stimulate budding, blooming and foliage green-up. Fish emulsion can be used as a liquid feed throughout the growing season, applied right over the mulch. Fish meal can be gently scratched into the soil. Epsom salts (magnesium sulfate) are a good source of magnesium and sulfur, which is essential for chlorophyll production. Epsom salts improve the production of blooms and boost the overall health of the plant.

Spraying the leaves with fertilizer is called foliar feeding. It won't provide all the nutrition a rose needs but is good for supplementing a soil fertility program. Foliar feeding is good for applying micronutrients. If your soil test reveals a need for micronutrients, a good form to use is chelated

Compost Tea Recipe

Mix a shovelful of compost in a 5-gallon (20-liter) bucket of water or a bucketful of compost in a 45-gallon (170-liter) barrel of water and let sit for a week. Dilute this mix, preferably with rainwater or filtered water, until it resembles weak tea.

micronutrients sprayed on the foliage and onto the soil. Do not apply foliar feeds if temperatures are 90° F (32° C) or higher.

HOW TO FERTILIZE

If you are unsure about how much fertilizer to use, it is better to apply a little less fertilizer and a little more water. Most importantly, never fertilize a dry plant! Water the plant very well the day before you plan to fertilize to reduce the potential of burning.

Follow the directions that came with the fertilizer. Always wear gloves when using granular fertilizers. If you are using granular fertilizers, measure the recommended amount and spread it out in a ring around the base of the rose and lightly scratch the fertilizer into the soil with a cultivator or rake. Leave a 6–8" (15–20 cm) diameter of unfertilized area directly around the base of the rose so the fertilizer can reach the feeder roots.

Liquid fertilizers are mixed with water and poured onto the rootzone or sprayed onto the foliage. Hose-end sprayers, available at garden centers, department stores and some nurseries, make applying liquid fertilizers easy. Many rosarians use both granular and liquid fertilizers in various combinations.

Pruning

Pruning is very important for roses. It is far better to prune a rose at least once a year than to not prune it at all. To prune effectively, you need to know why you are pruning, when to prune, how and where to make proper cuts, how to prune the specific rose you are growing and how to clean up after you are done.

Pruning removes any dead, diseased, damaged, interfering, crossing or rubbing canes. Pruning shapes the rose and keeps the center open to allow good air circulation. Pruning also keeps large roses from growing out of bounds.

The natural growth habit for roses is to send suckers up from the base of the plant. These shoots are vigorous and productive for a few years and then they lose their vigor. The rose then channels its energy into producing new vigorous shoots. The older shoots still produce flowers, but they are small and of poor quality. Removing the older shoots allows the rose to channel all its energy into the new shoots and large, robust flowers.

WHEN TO PRUNE

The best time to prune most roses is in late winter or early spring just before the rose breaks winter dormancy, or about 30 days before the last spring frost date. Your local garden center should be able to provide information on the last spring frost date for your area. If there is a chance of a late cold snap, it is better to delay your pruning so any new tender growth will not be damaged by frost. Do not prune in late summer or fall because pruning stimulates new growth that can be winter killed. Uncover your roses and level the soil before you begin pruning.

Unhilling the rose with a hoe before spring pruning

Using a stick to aid in unhilling

Uncovered rose is ready to prune

The hybrid tea at the front of the bed has been pruned.

A bed of hybrid teas after pruning

Once-blooming roses, such as old garden roses or species roses, are not pruned in early spring. Instead they are pruned after flowering is finished. Because these roses bloom mostly or entirely on two-year-old wood, pruning them in spring would remove the wood that produces flowers. Repeat bloomers should be pruned after the last flush or in spring. Once-flowering climbers can have flowering canes removed completely after flowering or the following spring.

Fall pruning should be done only to prepare the rose for winter. Any fall pruning should occur after several hard frosts but before winter sets in. In areas with high winter winds, some roses, bush roses in particular, are pruned in fall to shorten the plant by one-third or down to knee height to help prevent wind rock, which occurs when the action of the wind moves the rose enough to loosen the roots from the rootzone. Even when the rose is hilled or covered up with soil, the wind movement of the long canes creates holes or cones in the soil where water or cold air can enter, causing winter damage. Canes may need to be shortened to fit inside any physical winter protection being used, such as a box or rose cone. Repeat-blooming roses, such as hybrid teas, grandifloras and floribundas, are sheared down to 18–24" (46–61 cm) in fall in preparation for winter, to make them easier to cover with protective mulch.

Many rosarians use the blooming of forsythia (picture above) to signal when to begin pruning. Forsythia is a shrub that produces golden yellow blooms when most other plants are still dormant.

EQUIPMENT FOR ROSE PRUNING
You will need the following tools to do a good pruning job:

Secateurs are hand pruners used for cutting canes up to ³/₄" (2 cm) diameter. Using secateurs for cutting canes larger than ³/₄" (2 cm) diameter increases the risk of damaging the remaining branch or stem and is physically more difficult for the person doing the pruning.

Loppers are long-handled pruners used for large, old canes up to 1¹/₂" (4 cm) diameter.

Pruning saws can also be used for removing large, old canes. The teeth are designed to cut through green wood. Select a saw that has a short blade, around 8" (20 cm), with a pointed tip and tapered blade for cutting in tight areas.

Puncture-proof leather gloves, preferably with leather extending up the forearm.

The cleaner and sharper the cut, the easier it is for the rose to heal, so make sure your tools are sharp and clean before you begin any pruning task. If the cane you are cutting is diseased, you must sterilize the tool between each cut. A solution of 1 part bleach and 9 parts water is an effective sterilizer. Hydrogen peroxide or isopropyl alcohol can be used instead of bleach.

Bypass (scissors-type) secateurs and loppers provide a cleaner cut than non-bypass models. Anvil-type pruners, which are non-bypass, cut like a cleaver and cutting board. The cuts from anvil pruners tend to be ragged, especially if the blade is dull.

IDENTIFYING BUD EYES

New shoots arise from the buds, or bud eyes, as well as from the base of the rose. Most pruning cuts will be made just above a bud. Buds are immediately above where a leaf was attached to the cane. At pruning time most buds are easily identified as little half-circle bulges on the cane. If the buds are a little hard to spot, especially on older canes, look for a horizontal, flat or crescent-shaped scar left by the leaf and assume a bud will develop just above it. New growth from buds occurs in the direction the bud is facing. When selecting a bud to cut back to, always select one that is on the side of the cane that faces away from the center of the plant. Your rose bush will have a nicer shape and you will keep the center of the rose bush open. Keeping the center of a rose clear allows air to flow through, which is a good defense against fungal diseases.

Latent buds, also known as dormant buds, are located on either side of a primary bud. They are stimulated when an actively growing cane is removed either deliberately or accidentally. They are easy to remove with your thumb if you want to direct more of the plant's energy to the primary bud. You might want to leave them because latent buds may need to develop to replace old canes that are removed.

François Juranville

Jens Munk

HOW TO PRUNE

In general, tender roses need more pruning and hardy roses need less. The following pruning is the minimum that all roses should have annually:

- Remove any dead, diseased, damaged or interfacing canes (canes crossing each other, rubbing together or growing into the center of the plant).
- If the rose is mature, remove two or so of the oldest, unproductive canes, but don't remove too many. Roses store a lot of energy in their canes in the form of unused nutrients and plant-produced sugars and proteins. If more of the canes remain after pruning, the rose will not have to rely so much on its roots to get going in spring.

If a rose has not been pruned for a few years and is gnarly and overgrown, don't cut it back all at once. Complete the task over two years, by removing no more than one-third per year, to lessen the shock for the plant. After the first pruning, there will still be foliage producing energy and food for the plant. Successive hard pruning stresses the plant and limits the growth of the root system, which in turn limits the new growth above the ground.

Every four to five years, prune to renew the rose's branch structure. Work with the rose's natural growth habit. You will get a nicer looking, healthier rose when you follow the basic shape of the plant rather than work against it.

PRUNING DIFFERENT VARIETIES

Roses that grow vigorously might benefit from additional pruning. A severe pruning every year is recommended for hybrid teas, grandifloras and floribundas. Ensure the center is

Pruning cuts for a hybrid tea

opened and a nice vase-shaped plant outline is created. **Hybrid teas** should be pruned to three to five buds on three to five well-spaced canes. White and yellow hybrid teas are generally less vigorous, so they should be pruned like floribundas and grandifloras. **Floribundas** and **grandifloras** should be pruned to five to seven buds on five to seven well-spaced canes.

Prune **miniatures** once they break dormancy, by at least one-half, removing all weak and twiggy growth and removing any extra long canes or winter damage. Some rosarians cut them back to the lowest outward-facing buds on the previous year's growth.

Pruning for **shrub** and **old garden roses** involves mostly thinning and shaping. Prune in spring; do not prune after flowering other than to deadhead. Choose the rose to fit the space rather than having to prune to

Pruning a floribunda

keep the rose within bounds. Generally you can prune, to the crown or base, up to one-quarter of the old, unproductive canes annually on mature plants. Remove thin and twiggy growth (less than $1/4$" or 6 mm

Pruning an old garden rose

Pruning cuts for a climber

in diameter) and all shoots lying on the ground. Shortening extra long canes on once-blooming varieties will stimulate flowering laterals.

Climbing roses should not be pruned for two to three years after planting to allow the rose to produce long canes from which the flowering lateral branches will develop. Canes should be trained into position as they grow and mature. There are two aims when pruning climbers— encouraging growth of flowering lateral branches and initiating new main canes to replace old, unproductive canes. Annually remove one or two of the oldest canes (older than three years) and trim lateral branches to retain two to three bud eyes per lateral. Long canes can be trimmed to keep them within bounds.

If a main cane is growing in the wrong direction, make every attempt to train it into place by bending it

and tying it to the support. If it does not want to cooperate, then remove the whole cane at the base. Long lateral branches may be treated as main canes.

After blooming, **rambling roses** produce many long, flexible canes from the base and long laterals from the canes that have just flowered. Next year's flowers arise from this new growth. Remove any canes that are not producing long, vigorous laterals after they have flowered.

Remove once-flowering canes to the base after flowering. Cut back laterals to 24–36" (61–91 cm) from the main stem.

For repeat-blooming ramblers, remove the flowering laterals to two to three buds from the main stem and remove one to two of the oldest canes to rejuvenate the rose. Train new canes to fill the space left from the removal of the old, unproductive

A floribunda rose before (left) and after (right) spring pruning

canes. Remove excess new growth from the base, but leave some growth to replace old canes.

Prune **groundcover roses** to keep them in the available space. If the groundcover rose is a creeping, stem-rooting variety, cut it well back from the boundary to an upward-facing bud or thin it out back to a main branch. Flower Carpet (p. 137) should be cut down to 10–12" (25–30 cm) to rejuvenate.

The goal for pruning **standard roses** is to have a nice balanced head.

Shorten shoots by one-third. Ensure that the head is not too large or heavy to be supported. For weeping standards, remove stems that have finished flowering and leave the current season's growth alone.

PROPER PRUNING CUTS

If pruning cuts are made correctly the plant heals quickly, preventing disease and insect attacks. Pruning cuts for roses include (1) shortening canes to a bud or a branch and (2) removing old canes at the base.

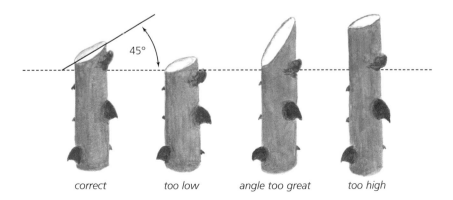

45°

correct   too low   angle too great   too high

Cutting back to a bud eye

Secateurs and loppers must be properly oriented when making a cut. The blade of the secateurs or loppers should be to the plant side of the cut and the hook should be to the side being removed. A cut made with the hook on the plant side will be ragged and difficult to heal.

When shortening a cane to a bud, the cut should be made to slightly less than 1/4" (6 mm) above a bud (see diagram on previous page). If the cut is too far away from or too close to the bud, the wound will not heal properly. Pay attention to the bud you are cutting back to. Cut to a bud that is pointing away from the center of the rose. Shortening a cane to a branch is similar to shortening a cane to a bud. It is healthiest for the rose if the diameter of the cane you are cutting is at least one-third of the diameter of the branch you are cutting back to. The cut should be made at slightly less than 1/4" (6 mm) above the lateral branch and lined up with the angle of the branch.

When removing an old cane at the base, always cut as close as you can to the base (or bud union if it is exposed). Any deadwood or stubs left on the rose are potential homes for insect pests and disease. In areas where there are rose cane borer attacks, the ends of the cut canes may be sealed with a little dab of white glue or pruning paste. Ensure the sealant is spread over the entire cut end. Sealants are unnecessary if borers are not a problem.

PEGGING DOWN

Pegging down is the process of bending rose canes and pegging them to the ground near the tip of the cane. It is a way of controlling or training roses without actually cutting them. Roses are genetically programmed to grow to a certain height. Pegging the canes down tricks the rose into thinking it must send out new growth to attain that height. This is good for roses with long, flexible canes, especially hybrid perpetual and bourbon roses that tend to bloom only at the tips of their canes. Pegging down promotes flower production along the length of the cane.

In late summer or early fall, gently bend the canes over, cut the tips back to the first upward-facing bud from the tip and peg the canes to the ground with long, stiff wire staples. You can use coat hangers bent in a U-shape or you can buy staples from a landscape supply business. Another method is to tie the canes to a low frame (no higher than 18" or 46 cm). The shoots created by pegging down should be pruned to 4–6" (10–15 cm) annually, in spring for repeat-blooming roses and after flowering for the once bloomers.

SPRING PRUNING IN COLD WINTER AREAS

In cold winter areas, the canes of only the hardiest roses survive above their protective cover or snowline. Prune in spring to remove winter-damaged wood back to healthy, out-ward-facing buds. Frost-damaged canes appear light brown to black with no green or reddish-brown color visible. Frost damage begins at the tip of the cane and works down, sometimes right to the base. The pith of frost-damaged wood is brown. Healthy wood has white or slightly green pith. In older canes healthy pith may be a little off-white.

Begin cutting at the top of the cane and work down until you encounter healthy wood. The correct way to proceed is little by little, to prevent the removal of too much healthy wood. If you are not sure whether the cane is alive, leave it alone until new growth begins so you can see exactly what is happening with the canes. Old canes of rugosa roses may look frost damaged but are often still alive.

AFTER-PRUNING CARE

After spring pruning, clean up around your roses. Remove any leaves remaining on the plant from the previous year. Clean up any debris and old leaves on the ground to remove insects and disease that may have overwintered there.

During spring cleanup, many rosarians spray their roses and the soil with a lime-sulfur or lime-sulfur-and-oil mix to destroy any insect eggs or disease spores that might still be there. Roses must still be dormant when applying this spray. If your rose has already broken dormancy and started to shoot, spray only lime sulfur, as dormant oil can damage the young shoots.

Pegging down

Suckers are growing to the left of this hybrid tea.

Removing Suckers

A sucker is a shoot that arises from a plant's roots or underground stems. For grafted roses a sucker is unwanted growth that arises from the rootstock below the bud union.

Watch for suckers throughout the growing season and remove them. They grow vigorously but do not flower, and they sap energy away from the variety above the graft union.

It's easy to spot suckers because the stem and foliage of the sucker will likely look different from the grafted variety. Remove a sucker and its latent buds by exposing the sucker where it attaches to the root and pulling it sharply away from the root. It's best to pull the suckers completely off the rootstock.

It is easiest to remove suckers when they are still small. If the sucker is too large to pull off without damaging the root, then prune it off the root if possible. This is a temporary solution, however, as it will grow back. Cultivating around the rootstock can also remove suckers, but be gentle. Standard roses tend to sucker along the stem. These suckers can be removed by hand.

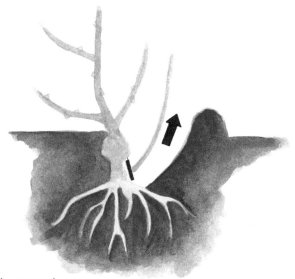

Pull a sucker off the rootstock.

Deadheading

Deadheading is the process of removing spent blooms. It helps to keep plants looking clean and tidy and, for repeat bloomers, it encourages more blooms. When a rose plant has finished flowering it naturally wants to produce seed-bearing hips, and when the rose is producing seed, it knows it doesn't need to produce any more flowers. Removing the old blooms encourages the formation of new flowers, as the energy that would have gone into seed production is redirected into new bloom production.

Remove the spent blooms as quickly as possible after they droop and fade. For large-flowered roses such as hybrid teas, cut the stem just above the first strong outward true leaf (five leaflets). The shoot that will emerge from the bud will grow outward, allowing for an open form that will improve air circulation and light penetration. The thicker the cane is where you make your deadheading cut, the stronger the new cane will be.

On weak canes or new plants, just snap off the bloom, retaining the maximum amount of foliage. This allows the canes to grow thicker and the plant to be healthier.

For cluster-flowered roses such as floribundas, remove the entire cluster to just above the first strong outward true leaf (five leaflets).

Stop deadheading in late summer or early fall, four to six weeks before the first frost date. This allows for hip production, which signals the plant to prepare for winter dormancy.

It is better to not deadhead once-blooming roses. Removing the flowers means no hips will be produced. Many once-blooming roses have attractive hips that provide good fall and winter color as well as food for birds and other wildlife.

Deadheading

Winter Protection

Whether you need to provide winter protection depends on where you live, the type of roses you are growing and where you have planted them. Cold air accumulates in low spots, depressions or the bottom of slopes, and roses planted in those areas might need extra protection. Areas that are exposed to winter winds will need protection, such as a temporarily erected screen. Tender roses such as hybrid teas, grandifloras or floribundas will require some form of protection. It is often not the winter cold that kills a rose but the freeze-and-thaw cycle that occurs when winter is ending and spring is beginning. It is said that roses with yellow and apricot-colored blooms suffer the most in winter and need extra protection. Many beautiful roses, such as the Explorer series or rugosa roses, need no protection at all.

Roses hilled for winter

The best way to have a rose survive winter is to plant one that is hardy for your area. If you grow tender roses, the following methods are effective for winter protection.

GARDEN ROSES

Stop fertilizing with nitrogen fertilizer after the second flush of blooms (but no later than the end of July) for repeat-blooming roses and after blooming for once-bloomers.

Stop deadheading four to six weeks before the first frost date.

Allow hips to develop so the rose begins preparing itself for the winter dormant season.

Maintain your watering right to freeze-up to prevent the roots from drying out during winter. The plant does not stop growing over winter, it just slows down.

As soon as frost kills the foliage, remove any remaining foliage and clean up the ground around the rose to eliminate overwintering sites for insect pests and disease spores.

Once the foliage is removed, cut the canes of hybrid teas, grandifloras and floribundas to 18" (46 cm). Cutting the canes back helps reduce wind rock (see p. 59).

Mound soil or other suitable insulating material over the crown and canes to a depth of 10–12" (25–30 cm). The mounding is to protect the crown or bud union. Give the mound a good soaking or tightly pack when hilling the soil with the back of a chop hoe or your hands. Some rosarians mound soil over the plant, surround the plant with a wire mesh screen and fill the remaining space with insulating material. This method takes extra work, but it works well in the coldest areas.

If there is snow in your area, keep the roses covered with it. Often only the canes above the snowline are killed.

Plastic cones for covering roses are commercially available. If you use a plastic cone, install it after the ground first freezes. Mound soil over the base of the rose as described above. Tie the rose canes together and cut them short enough to fit inside the cone. Cover the lip at the bottom of the cone with soil to keep the cone in place. Place a brick or stone on top of the cone for extra weight. Ensure that air is able to circulate in the cone on warm days. Some rose growers drill a few holes in the top of the cone and others cut the top of the cone off to make a removable lid. Cold frames to protect larger roses can be built from plywood or rigid Styrofoam or polyfoam insulation. The cold frame should have a lid that can be opened on warm days.

Adelaide Hoodless

CONTAINER ROSES

To protect container roses, use one of the following methods:

Move the container to an area that stays just around freezing but no colder than 23° F (−5° C), such as a heated garage or cold room in the house. Make sure the area does not get too warm or you might stimulate unwanted growth. Water the container thoroughly before you bring it in and not again until spring, unless it dries out completely.

OR

Bury the rose, container and all. Dig a hole large enough to lay the container and rose on its side in the hole. Backfill the hole, ensuring the container and rose are completely covered with soil. Mark the spot so you can find it easily in spring. You may also bury the container upright with the rose exposed and follow the above method for protecting roses in the garden.

TREE ROSES

Tree roses need to have two bud unions protected, and one of the unions is well off the ground. The common protection method is to wrap the head of the rose plant in burlap. Another way to protect tree roses is to grow them in containers and take them into a protected area in winter. Another method is to dig out the rose, dig a trench and bury the tree rose horizontally in the soil and mound with extra soil. Make sure to mark its location.

CLIMBERS AND RAMBLERS

Protecting tender climbers and ramblers requires a fair amount of work. You can gently remove all the canes from their support and bury them in a trench, ensuring you also bury the crown of the plant. The trench can be long and narrow or just large enough to fit the coiled canes. Another method is to leave the canes where they are and wrap them in a couple of layers of burlap. The base of the rose will still need to be protected or hilled up with soil and mulch. In warmer areas of the province, hilling the roses is all that is necessary. There may be some dieback during severe winters, but new canes will shoot from the base.

City of York

UNCOVERING YOUR ROSES

Different parts of your garden will heat up at different rates. Monitor your roses. As soon as you see new growth, remove the protection. Weak and spindly growth is possible if you wait too long before removing your winter protection. Many rosarians remove winter protection from their roses when they see the leaf buds of their local native trees beginning to break (swell and grow).

When uncovering roses, carefully use a chop hoe to remove the soil or mulch to avoid damaging any new growth. Do not graze the canes or knock off any shoots. If there is a risk of late frost, the rose can be covered with a sheet or blanket. Remove any dead leaves or debris from the area as part of your spring cleanup.

Hilled-up material can be dug back into the soil to help reduce compaction, the compressing of soil air-pockets caused by heavy foot traffic especially in wet weather. The air-pockets, more commonly known by rosarians as soil micro or macro pores, are tributaries that carry water and nutrients throughout the soil. Rose roots, like all other roots, need air to breathe. Mulching the rose beds, reducing foot traffic during wet weather and digging in hilled amendments helps to reduce compaction.

If leaves and straw were used to protect your roses, compost the material after uncovering the roses.

Propagation

If you have developed a passion for growing roses, you may want to move to the next level and begin propagating your own roses. There are many reasons to propagate your own roses, including developing new varieties and sharing roses with other gardeners. Following are brief discussions of some of the techniques used to propagate more plants. More information can be found in other print sources. See the Resources on page 262.

Roses are propagated by budding, cuttings, seed or, for some roses, ground layering. Budding is the most common means of commercially propagating roses. To simplify, budding is the process of inserting a leaf bud of one rosebush under the bark of a rootstock variety. It has to be done in a very particular manner and requires practice.

Seed propagation requires time and patience. When creating a new variety, rose breeders pollinate one rose variety with pollen from another and grow hybrid plants from the resulting seeds. This is known as hybridizing.

The process of seeding roses is similar to seeding any perennial or woody ornamental, with the seeds of roses taken from the ripe hips. Seeding most often results in variable seedlings, with different colors, forms and so on, depending on the parentage used.

Roses grown from cuttings are genetically identical to the plant the cuttings were taken from, so propagating by cuttings is used when you want more of a certain variety of rose. Patented roses are protected by plant patent laws and must not be reproduced by any means.

Ground layering allows future cuttings to form their own roots before they are removed from the parent plant. A section of a flexible branch is buried until it produces roots, at which time it is removed from the parent plant. This method works well with lax-stemmed roses such as albas, damasks, bourbons and some species roses.

If you have own-root roses, you can take advantage of the naturally occurring suckers. Let the sucker grow until it develops roots of its own. The sucker can then be removed and planted to a new location. It's kind of like automatic ground layering without all the work.

Handel

Problems & Pests

There is both good and bad when it comes to roses and pests and diseases. Many insects and diseases attack only one plant species while others, such as aphids, have a variety of hosts. Mixed plantings can make it more difficult for pests to find their preferred hosts and establish a population. At the same time, because roses are in the same spot for many years, problems can become permanent. The advantage is that beneficial insects, birds and other pest-devouring organisms can also develop permanent populations.

For many years pest control meant spraying or dusting, with the goal to eliminate every pest in the landscape. A more moderate approach is known as IPM (Integrated Pest Management or Integrated Plant Management). The goal of IPM is to reduce pest problems to levels at which only negligible damage is done, by incorporating cultural, physical, biological and, lastly, chemical means of control. Of course, gardeners must determine what degree of damage is acceptable to them. Someone growing hybrid tea roses for exhibition will tolerate far less damage than someone growing species roses in a woodland garden. Consider whether a pest's damage is localized or covers the entire plant. Will the damage kill the plant or is it affecting only the outward appearance? Are there methods of controlling the pests without chemicals?

Chemical controls should always be the last resort. They can endanger the gardener and his or her family and pets and can kill as many good organisms as bad, leaving the garden more vulnerable. A good IPM program includes learning about your plants, the conditions they need for healthy growth, what pests might affect them, where and when to look for those pests and how to control them. Keep records of pest damage because your observations can reveal patterns useful in

Japanese beetles

spotting recurring problems and in planning your maintenance regime.

Proper identification of what is affecting your rose will help you take appropriate corrective measures. Insects, disease or nutrient deficiencies can cause problems. If you are unsure what is happening to your rose, contact the local rose society or your local garden center for advice. Post-secondary schools and the internet are other good sources for information.

Choose roses of top quality that are resistant to the major diseases in your area. Many beautiful disease-resistant varieties are available. (See p. 93 for a list of disease-resistant roses.) Hybridizers are working at breeding back in the resistance that was being somewhat lost in the quest for the perfect flower form. If you want to grow roses that are susceptible to disease, you may need to tolerate a less-than-perfect rose or find a way to minimize the damage. A good way to determine which roses are the best for your garden is to contact a local rose society. Consulting rosarians are often available to help you with your selection needs. Another way is to visit a local rose garden or walk through your neighborhood and see for yourself which roses are growing well.

There are four steps in effective and responsible pest management. Cultural controls are the most important. Physical controls should be attempted next, followed by biological controls. Resort to chemical controls only when the first three possibilities have been exhausted.

Leaves afflicted with blackspot

Cultural controls are the gardening techniques you use in the daily care of your garden. They include ensuring that the rose has adequate light, water and air circulation. Provide adequate drainage and plenty of organic matter and nutrients with an ideal soil pH. Prevent the spread of disease and insects by keeping gardening tools clean. Thoroughly clean and remove fallen leaves and dead plant matter throughout the season, especially in fall. Providing the conditions roses need for healthy growth reduces plant stress. A stressed plant is vulnerable to pests and disease.

Physical controls are generally used to combat insect problems. An example of such a control is picking insects off plants by hand, which is not as daunting as it may seem if you catch the problem when it is just beginning. Simply squishing the insects is another method. Other physical controls include barriers that stop insects from getting to the plant, and traps that catch or confuse insects. Physical control of diseases often necessitates removing the infected plant part or parts to prevent the spread of the problem. Burn the infected material or take it to a permitted disposal site.

Biological controls make use of populations of predators that prey on pests. Birds, snakes, frogs, spiders, lady beetles and certain bacteria can play an important role in keeping pest populations at a manageable level. Encourage these creatures to take up permanent residence in your garden. A birdbath and birdfeeder will encourage birds to enjoy your yard and feed on a variety of insect pests. Beneficial insects are probably already living in your landscape, and you can encourage them to stay by planting appropriate food sources. Many beneficial insects eat nectar from flowers such as perennial yarrow. Biological insects are available for purchase from various organic control suppliers as well.

Chemical controls should be used only as the last alternative to pest and disease management, but if you must use them there are some 'organic' options available. Organic sprays are no less dangerous than chemical ones, but they will break down into harmless compounds. The main drawback to using any chemicals is that they may also kill the beneficial

Frogs eat many insect pests.

The foliage of this Alba Meidiland has blackspot.

insects you have been trying to attract to your garden. Organic chemicals are available at most garden centers. Follow the manufacturer's instructions carefully and apply no more than the recommended rate. Note that if a particular pest or disease is not listed on the package, it will not be controlled by that product. Proper and early identification is vital to finding a quick solution. When using any chemicals, including pesticides, insecticides and fungicides, alternate different spray products so the pest won't build up a resistance to the chemical.

Whereas cultural, physical, biological and chemical controls are all possible defenses against insects, many diseases can only truly be controlled culturally. It is most often weakened plants that succumb to diseases. Healthy plants can often fight off illness, although some diseases can infect plants regardless

of their level of health. In that case, prevention is often the only hope. If a plant has been infected, remove the infected leaves and prune out infected branches immediately.

Fungicides

You can apply fungicides as a preventive measure when conditions are right for disease growth or after you see the disease on your rose. You can choose between organic and chemical fungicides. Both are effective, but organic fungicides are far better for the environment. If you feel a need to use chemical fungicides, check with the local garden center or rose society to acquire the appropriate information. At all times follow the directions on the product label. And remember: more is not better.

The following is a list of fungicides that when used responsibly have no adverse effects on the environment.

Baking soda & horticultural oil

University testing has confirmed the effectiveness of this mixture against powdery mildew.

In a spray bottle, mix:

4 teaspoons (20 ml) baking soda

1 tablespoon (15 ml) horticultural oil

1 gallon (4 l) water

Spray the foliage lightly, including the undersides. Do not pour or spray this mix directly into the soil.

Baking soda & citrus oil

The following mixture treats both blackspot and powdery mildew.

In a spray bottle, mix:

4 teaspoons (20 ml) baking soda

1 tablespoon (15 ml) citrus oil

1 gallon (4 l) water

Spray the foliage lightly, including the undersides. Do not pour or spray this mix directly into the soil.

Garlic spray

This spray is an effective, organic means of controlling aphids, leafhoppers, whiteflies and some fungi and nematodes.

Soak:

6 tablespoons (90 ml) finely minced garlic in 2 teaspoons (10 ml) mineral oil for a minimum of 24 hours

Add:

1 pint of water and $1^1/_2$ teaspoons (7.5 ml) of liquid dish soap

Stir and strain into a glass container for storage. Combine 1–2 tablespoons of this concentrate with 2 cups (500 ml) water to make a spray. Test the spray on a couple of leaves and check after two days for any damage from the soap/garlic mixture. If there is no damage, then you can spray your rose thoroughly, ensuring good coverage of the foliage.

Milk spray

Milk spray helps prevent and control blackspot and mildew. It has been tested on roses and a variety of vegetables and has been moderately successful. Any kind of milk can be used, from high fat milk to skim and even powdered milk. Milk with a lower fat content is recommended as it will have less of an odor. Mix one part milk with nine parts water and apply in a spray every five to seven days for a total of three applications.

Fish emulsion/seaweed (kelp)

These products are usually used as foliar nutrient feeds but appear to also work against fungal diseases by either preventing the fungus from spreading to non-infected areas or by changing the growing conditions for the fungus.

Neem oil

Neem oil is derived from the neem tree (from India) and is used as an insecticide, miticide and fungicide. It is most effective when used as a preventive measure. Apply when conditions are favorable for disease development. Neem is virtually harmless to most beneficial insects and microorganisms.

Antitranspirants

These products were developed to reduce water transpiration, or loss of water, in plants. The waxy polymers also surround fungal spores, preventing the spread of spores to nearby leaves and stems. When applied according to label directions, antitranspirants are environmentally friendly.

Sulfur and lime-sulfur

These products work well as preventive measures. You can get ready-made products or wettable powders that you mix yourself. Do not spray when the temperature is expected to be 90° F (32° C) or higher as doing so can damage the plant.

Bordo or Bordeaux Fungicides

These products can be used to treat fungal problems including blackspot, powdery mildew and rust. They are available in wettable powders and are easily applied either dry or wet. Follow the recommended rates and instructions to prevent the foliage from being burned.

Be careful if you are using copper mixtures, including Bordo or Bordeaux fungicides. They may effectively control fungal disease for the entire season but can be damaging to the soil and toxic to the user.

Many consumers are demanding effective pest products that do not harm the environment. Biopesticides are made from plants, animals, bacteria and minerals. Microbial pesticides contain microbes such as bacteria, fungi, viruses and other microbes as the active ingredient. Plant pesticides are derived from naturally occurring plant compounds. Biochemical pesticides come from other naturally occurring substances that control pests by non-toxic means. They are much less harmful than conventional pesticides and for the most part target only the pest. They are effective in small quantities and they decompose quickly in the environment. These products should reduce the reliance on chemical pesticides.

Glossary of Pests & Diseases

The following glossary includes brief descriptions of some of the pests and diseases that may occur. You might want to further explore identification of pests and their life-cycles, their most damaging stage and the best methods of reducing damage. Check the list of resources on page 262 or contact your local library, rose or garden club for additional information.

Do not be discouraged after reading this section. You may never encounter any of these problems (blackspot and aphids are the most common). Remember that your best defense against any pest or disease is a healthy rose.

Aphids

APHIDS

Tiny, pear-shaped insects, winged or wingless; black, brown, green, red or gray. Cluster along stems, buds and leaves but are most often found on new, tender growth. Suck sap from plants; cause distorted or stunted growth. Aphids produce honeydew, a sticky, sugary fluid deposited on leaves and stems. Sticky honeydew forms on surfaces and encourages the growth of black sooty mold. Aphids are like 'plant lice' and are the most common of rose insect pests and likely the easiest to eradicate.

What to Do. Squish small colonies by hand; dislodge them with brisk water spray; spray serious infestations with insecticidal soap; many predatory insects and birds feed on them. An application of dormant oil will kill overwintering eggs.

ARMILLARIA ROOT ROT (SHOESTRING FUNGUS, OAK ROOT FUNGUS)

Soil-borne, parasitic fungus; causes decay of roots and crown by breaking down tissue. May kill the plant quickly or slowly. Plants exhibit stunted growth. Leaves turn yellow or brown; plant wilts, then dies, often one stem or branch at a time. White fungal strands appear under the bark near the crown and on the roots. Honey-colored mushrooms appear around the base of the plant during wet weather. Attacks are most frequent in heavy, clay soils with poor drainage. It is most harmful and prevalent in oaks. Weakened or stressed plants are also vulnerable.

What to Do. Avoid planting susceptible varieties where the fungus is known to exist. Ensure good surface and sub-surface drainage. When preparing a planting area, remove all old tree and shrub roots and mix in a large amount of rich compost. Remove and destroy infected plants; replant only resistant plants.

BACTERIAL CANKER

Enters the rose through wounded stem tissue and can attack any part of the rose. Weakened roses more susceptible. Red or yellow spots on the stem progress to form brown patches and lesions that shrivel and die. If the disease is severe enough it will girdle the stem, killing all growth above the infected area.

What to Do. Maintain plant vigor. Avoid wounds on plants. Control borers. Prune out and destroy diseased branches (see Pruning, p. 58). Sterilize your pruning equipment after each cut. Remove rubbing or crossing branches annually.

Japanese beetles destroy leaves and blooms.

BEETLES

Many types and sizes; usually round with hard, shell-like outer wings covering membranous inner wings. Some types are beneficial, e.g., ladybird beetles ('ladybugs'); others are not. Both the adult insects and the larvae may feed on roses and other plants. Japanese Beetle skeletonizes leaves and occasionally feeds on the inside of the blooms, which makes them difficult to control. Rose Chafer destroys buds. Rose Curculio, sometimes known as Rose Weevil, drills holes in the buds. Cucumber Beetle feeds on the petals. Larvae feed on roots and other organic materials in the soil. June Beetle larvae can cause root damage. All of these overwinter in the soil, so the soil itself may need treatment.

What to Do. Remove by hand and drop in a container of soapy water. Spread an old sheet under the rose plant and shake off beetles to collect and dispose of them. Spray insecticidal soap or pyrethrin (plant-based insecticides) on visible insects. Plant repellent herbs and perennials as companions—catmint, chamomile, garlic, lavender, rosemary, garden sage, painted daisy, tansy and thyme. Plant radishes to attract beetles away from roses. Treat soil with parasitic nematodes, spray roses with beneficial insect sprays, repellents like garlic water, neem oil and other registered pesticides or beneficial bacteria. Milky spore is effective on Japanese Beetle larvae and Rose Chafer larvae but may take up to three years of applications for complete control. Kill larvae with diatomaceous earth. Dust with Rotenone. Prune out infected portions and destroy. Use traps to catch Japanese Beetles.

Rose heavily afflicted with blackspot

BLACKSPOT

The most prevalent fungal disease for roses. The fungus overwinters in infected leaves and canes, so plant sanitation is important. Most problematic when warm, humid weather (70°–80° F or 21°–27° C) is sustained for over a week. Can cause weak growth and stems to die back. An infestation by a single spore can produce visible colonies in as little as 15 days. First appears on the lower foliage as black or brown blotches; yellow rings form to outline the blotches. Severely infected foliage drops; severe cases can defoliate a rose.

What to Do. Keep the area free of fallen infected leaves. Remove all the leaves before winterizing to prevent overwintering spores. Use a preventive fungicide when the environmental conditions are favorable to fungal infection. The spores are too small to see before they infect the leaf. Take extra care to spray the undersides of the leaves. Funginex and Daconil are common and effective chemical controls when all else fails.

BOTRYTIS

Fungal disease especially common in high humidity. Affects the stems and flowers of mature roses and the bare roots of poorly stored or shipped plants. Grayish-brown fuzzy mold on stems and flower buds; grayish-brown lesion runs down one side of the bud and onto the stem. Flower buds may not open or if they open partially the petal edges may appear soft and brown.

What to Do. Plant the rose where the morning sun can dry the plant; remove and destroy any infected plant parts. Improve the air circulation around and through the plant. Do not mulch over the crown. The commercially available chemical product Daconil has been effective.

CANE BORERS

Larvae of different insects. White to yellow and worm-like. Burrow into new and freshly cut canes. Destroy vascular tissue (plant veins and arteries) and structural strength. The stems die back from the tips. Look for small hole in the tip of the cane and a swollen band of tissue circling the cane at the bottom of the dieback. Split canes lengthwise with a knife to expose the borer.

What to Do. Handpick visible larvae and drop into a bucket of soapy water. Cut out and destroy infected canes. Do not put cut canes in the compost. Seal the ends of pruned canes with a drop of white glue or a plant wound–sealing product.

CATERPILLARS

Larvae of butterflies, moths, sawflies. Include budworms, cutworms, leaf rollers, corn earworms, rose slugs and webworms. Chew foliage and buds. Can completely defoliate a plant if infestation severe.

What to Do. Remove plant. Use high-pressure water and soap or pick caterpillars off by hand. Cut off and burn large tents or webs of larvae. Control biologically using the naturally occurring soil bacterium

Disinfecting Tools

Dip pruning tools into denatured alcohol or a solution of 10 percent liquid chlorine bleach and water. Disinfect tools between each plant when pruning non-infected plants; between each cut when pruning infected plants. After disinfecting tools, scrub any discolored areas with steel wool, sharpen cutting edges and oil metal surfaces.

Bacillus thuringiensis var. *kurstaki*, or *B.t.* for short (commercially available), which breaks down gut lining of caterpillars. Apply dormant oil in spring. Plants such as cornflower, purple coneflower or passion vine will attract the caterpillars away from roses; use neem oil or organic and synthetic pesticides; release parasitic wasps; encourage predatory insects with nectar plants such as yarrow. Diatomaceous earth is an effective control. Chemical controls include Rotenone.

CROWN GALL

Unusual wart-like swellings of plant tissues caused by bacteria; more prevalent on grafted roses; disease begins at the base of the plant or on the bud union. Bacteria in the soil enter through wounds in the root and crown. Makes tissue green and pliable before forming into dark, crusty growths on roots or crown. Stunts growth, restricts water and nutrient uptake and reduces foliage and bloom production. Easily spread by infected tools.

What to Do. Remove any plants that have galls. Replace contaminated soil. Some report success with pruning away galls and spraying the infected area with antibacterial solutions or copper compounds.

DEER, RABBITS

Eat roses and can cause significant damage, especially in rural areas.

What to Do. To repel deer, place soap on stakes or in suspended bags throughout your garden and mist the bags early in the evening. Fill mesh bags or nylon stockings with human hair and place in the affected

Powdery mildew

areas. Natural spray repellents, which should also work against rabbits, include egg and water mixed with an antidesiccant; bloodmeal solution; garlic oil solution. Fences to keep rabbits out must be buried deep into the ground to prevent the rabbits from burrowing underneath. A sprinkler activated by a motion sensor scares most wildlife away.

LEAF CUTTER BEE

Cuts neat, smooth circles from the edges of leaves.

What to Do. Nothing. It is a beneficial insect as a pollinator. Damage is only aesthetic.

LEAFHOPPERS

Small, wedge-shaped insects, often green, but can be brown, gray or multi-colored. Jump around frantically when disturbed. Suck juice from plant leaves and cause distorted growth. Can transmit diseases from plant to plant as they feed.

What to Do. Encourage predators by planting nectar-producing plants. Wash insects off with strong spray of water; spray with insecticidal soap.

MILDEW

Two types, both caused by fungus, but with different symptoms. *Downy mildew:* may be confused with blackspot. One of the most feared rose diseases, although rare; prefers cool, moist or humid conditions with splashing water and wind to carry its spores to the next host. Two days of dry, hot weather (90° F or 30° C or higher) will stop the disease, but spores remain for future infections. Purple-red irregular blotches on the new leaf and stem growth are systemic; lesions are a sign that the disease has spread throughout the plant. Gray fuzz on undersides of the foliage. *Powdery mildew:* attacks many rose varieties in all climates but prefers warm, moist, cloudy days and cool, humid nights. Less destructive than downy mildew. Appears on young leaves, stems and thorns. Begins as pinkish lesions and changes into a white or gray powdery coating. Canes can become distorted and flower petals appear dry and become discolored on the edges. Severe infestations may lead to new growth being distorted and dying.

What to Do. Choose roses that are not susceptible to mildew. Fall cleanup is essential to prevent mildew overwintering on canes and fallen leaves. Provide good air circulation. Remove and destroy any infected foliage. Apply fungicides such as lime-sulfur or dormant oil while the rose is dormant in spring. Other effective fungicides are Bordo or Bordeaux. Spray the soil as well to decrease overwintering active spores. There is no chemical control.

MOSSY ROSE GALL

Golf ball–sized, spiny balls on leaves or stems. Caused by *Diplolepis spinosa*, a cynipid gall wasp. Insect larvae develop inside the gall; adult wasps emerge the following spring. The galls are unsightly, alter the plant's shape and stress the host plant by taking nutrients away from

Insecticidal soap recipe
You can make your own insecticidal soap. Mix 1 teaspoon (5 ml) of mild dish detergent or pure soap (biodegradable options are available) with 1 quart (1 liter) of water in a clean spray bottle. Spray the surface areas of your plants and rinse them well within one hour of spraying.

the plant. Large numbers of galls on a plant can kill the plant.

What to Do. After the leaves drop in fall, prune the infested branches, cutting below the gall and above a bud, and destroy. For leaf galls, pick up fallen leaves in fall.

NEMATODES

Tiny worms that cannot be seen with the naked eye; give plants disease symptoms. Plant growth is stunted and does not respond to water or fertilizer. Roots have tiny bumps, galls or knots.

What to Do. Mulch soil, add lots of organic matter, clean up debris in fall. Can add parasitic nematodes to soil or treat soil with neem. Remove infected plants in extreme cases. Plant nematode-resistant plants.

ROOT ROT

Fungus that can cause weak, stunted growth. Leaves yellow and plant wilts and dies. Digging up plant will show rotted roots.

What to Do. Keep soil well drained. Do not overwater. Don't damage plant if you are digging around it; keep mulches away from plant base. Destroy plant if whole plant infected.

ROSE MIDGE

Small, nearly invisible adult insects; hatch at the growing tips and use their rasping mouth parts to feed on tender new tissue, especially flower buds. Rose shrivels or bears no flowers but the rest of the plant is healthy. Other evidence is scorched or blackened newer growth, blind tips and no buds. The symptoms are most evident in May and early June. Rose midge overwinters in soil.

What to Do. Difficult to control. Prune out and destroy blackened buds and canes; make sure to prune back hard to get rid of larvae that may have traveled down the cane. Add predatory nematodes to the soil to destroy the pupating larvae. Place a sheet of black plastic around the base of the rose to stop the larvae from reaching the soil to pupate. Keep the area around the plant free of weeds and litter. Consult a local rosarian, garden center or nursery for other solutions.

ROSE MOSAIC

Viral disease. Often confused with a nutrient deficiency causing interveinal yellowing. Yellow, irregular rings, line or netting patterns appear on leaf. Weakens plant, making it vulnerable to other pests and environmental stresses. Blooms may be distorted or undersized; may be early leaf drop. Not transmitted by insects or pruning tools.

What to Do. Remove the rose and replace the soil. Inform the people who sold you the plant that the plant had a virus. Contact suppliers to check if there have been reports of infected stock. Reputable suppliers will give you this information.

Leaves with rose mosaic virus

ROSE ROSETTE

Rare viral disease; no known cure; 100 percent fatal. Can be transmitted through infected rootstock. Mites may carry the disease; visible in the top few inches of new growth, usually near the bud eyes. Unusually dense prickles form on overly large, deep red or purple canes. New foliage appears distorted and crinkled and deep red or purple. Leaf stems are often flattened. Weak, chlorotic stems grow.

What to Do. Remove the cane to which any infected stem is attached. If other canes on the same plant become infected, remove the entire plant. The disease does not spread rapidly. Pruning will not transmit the disease. The use of predatory mites and neem oil may be effective.

ROSE SAWFLY LARVAE

Also called rose slugs; $1/2$" (13 mm) long green worms that coil into tight circle. Slug-like larvae that skeletonize foliage; especially destructive early in the growing season; remain on the underside of the leaves.

What to Do. Remove by hand (wear gloves—handling these pests can severely irritate skin); shake the larvae from the shrub and step on them. Spray with insecticidal soap or dust with pyrethrin to control severe infestations.

Rose hip covered in rust

RUST

Bright orange spots on leaf undersides; brown spots on upper leaf surfaces. Severe infestations appear as lesions and attack stems, and new growth becomes distorted. Can cause complete defoliation if left unchecked. More common in mild, wet weather (65°–70° F or 18°–21° C) including humid and foggy days and heavy morning dew. Spores are transmitted by wind and water and will overwinter. No roses are immune.

What to Do. Pick off and destroy infected leaves. Where the disease is common, spray weekly with sulfur in early spring. Prune at least 1" (2.5 cm) beyond the infected tissue.

SPIDER MITES

Tiny; eight-legged relatives of spiders; do not eat insects but may spin webs. Almost invisible to the naked eye; red, yellow or green; usually found on underside of leaves. Suck juice out of leaves; may see fine webbing on leaves and stems; may see mites moving on leaf undersides. Leaves become discolored and speckled; then turn brown and shrivel up. Spider mites prefer hot, dry weather; roses next to walls and those under drought stress are vulnerable to attack. Severe infestations can completely defoliate the plant.

What to Do. Wash off with strong water spray, especially targeting the undersides of leaves, until all signs of infestation are gone; predatory mites are available through garden centers; spray plants with insecticidal soap; ensure roses receive a deep and thorough watering as water-stressed plants are inviting to these creatures; special miticides (insecticide specific to mites) are available.

THRIPS

Tiny, flying insects. Scrape the flower surfaces and suck the juice from the open wounds. Damage is mainly on buds and open blooms. Petals appear bruised and discolored with light brown, translucent spots especially around the petal edges. Flowers can be deformed and buds can fail to open. Thrips seem to prefer tight, full buds of large-flowered yellow, pink or white roses. They thrive in hot and dry weather.

What to Do. Remove and destroy infected plant parts; encourage native predatory insects; spray serious infestations with insecticidal soap. Spunbound polyester covers can be effective.

WHITEFLIES

Tiny, white insects that flutter up into the air when the plant is disturbed. May appear as white dust above the foliage; tend to live near the top of the plant. Pierce the tissue and suck plant juices, causing yellowed

Ladybird beetle

leaves and weakened plants; produce honeydew. Damage may also include loss of foliage and stunted growth.

What to Do. Destroy weeds where insects may live. Encourage predatory insects and parasitic wasps. Spray severe infestations with insecticidal soap. Can use sticky traps, pheromone traps or light traps. Organic pesticides such as neem oil, horticultural oil and garlic water may be used.

Other problems
BALLING

Flowers open only partially; petal edges turn brown and rot. Occurs in high humidity and when overwatering from above. Some roses more susceptible than others, especially large blooms with thin petals or roses in shade. Balling blooms feel slimy and smell like decomposing organic matter. May also be caused by aphids, so keep aphid populations to a minimum.

What to Do. Difficult to control, caused by wet conditions. Prune out down to the first outward-facing true leaf.

BLIND SHOOTS

Sometimes shoots will arise that have no terminal flower buds. These are known as blind shoots. They take energy away from flower production.

What to Do. Cut back blind shoots to the first five-leaflet leaf with an outward-facing bud and hope it produces a flowering shoot. If you prefer, you can leave the blind shoots alone to retain more foliage.

HEAT STRESS

Major cause of yellowing leaves. Most noticeable during sudden temperature changes, especially on young plants and new growth. Leaf margins may scorch. Blooms may have darkened petal edges.

What to Do. Spray antitranspirants/antidesiccants; screen new plants from the sun; plant roses out of the afternoon sun; apply mulch to keep roots cool; run overhead sprinkler during the heat of the day.

MECHANICAL PROBLEMS

Cultivating too close to roots can damage them, and if roots are damaged, water and nutrient uptake is reduced and suckers are encouraged. A sign of damaged roots is yellowing foliage. If any roots are visible after cultivating, cover them.

What to Do. Take care when cultivating, going no deeper than 1–2" (2.5–5 cm); prune freshly exposed roots and replant; water deeply so roots penetrate below normal cultivation depths.

SALT STRESS

Accumulated salts compete with rose roots for moisture and can make required nutrients unavailable to plants (nutrient fixation), even though the nutrient is in the soil. The result is yellowed leaves, reduced plant growth, scorched leaf margins and eventually plant death. Container roses are most susceptible. The regular use of water-soluble fertilizers may lead to salt buildup, especially where soils are heavy or where irrigation or rainfall fails to wash these salts past the rootzone. Water high in phosphates may also cause salt buildup.

What to Do. Irrigate deeply; improve drainage; get soil tests done regularly; change soil in containers every three to four years.

WATER STRESS

Excess water: veins in the leaves begin to turn yellow first then the entire leaf yellows and droops; blooms fail to open completely; pith becomes soft and brown. *Inadequate water:* leaf margins wilt and scorch.

What to Do. Improve drainage; increase or decrease water as needed.

Nutrient Deficiencies

Sometimes what may look like pest or disease damage may be a nutrient deficiency or toxicity. A soil test or a plant tissue test is the only way to tell for sure if there is a nutrient deficiency or toxicity. See Soil Testing (p. 264) for locations.

Boron is responsible for water movement within the plant. A deficiency manifests itself as mottled, yellow, misshapen new leaves and buds that are growing too close to each other at the top of the plant.

Calcium deficiency occurs in younger or upper leaves. Leaves brown, curl, shrivel and die. Phosphorus and iron aren't available to the plant when there is an excess of calcium. Calcium is a nutrient in liming materials used to increase soil pH.

Iron deficiency, or iron chlorosis, is seen as interveinal yellowing of younger leaves at the top of the plant and the new growth. Iron contributes to the production of chlorophyll, essential for photosynthesis.

Magnesium deficiency looks like iron deficiency, but the yellow leaves with dark veins occur on the older lower leaves first. Magnesium is a common nutrient in some liming materials used to increase soil pH.

Manganese is responsible for metabolic processes. Without enough manganese, the smaller leaf veins stay green but the younger leaves appear webbed or net-like. The new leaves may be spotted and older leaves mottled. Excess manganese reduces iron uptake.

Nitrogen encourages vegetative growth. It is responsible for a plant's lush green growth and overall size. It is the nutrient most commonly deficient owing to leaching, especially from sandy soils. Nitrogen deficiency appears as undersized, pale green to yellow leaves, affecting the older leaves first. Stems may be weak and thin and blooms may be small. Overall plant growth is slow and stunted. Excess nitrogen causes overly lush dark green growth and weak stems susceptible to disease, winter kill and attack by insects.

Phosphorus encourages root development and is very rarely deficient. A phosphorus deficiency begins as dark green to purplish coloration in the older, lower leaves. Plant growth is stunted and spindly. Phosphorus toxicity appears as yellowing of the leaves between the veins. The leaves may be thicker, stems may be shorter and buds may be malformed or curled. Phosphorus accumulates in the soil, especially heavy soils.

Potassium promotes flowering, plant strength and structure so improves resistance to potential problems. It contributes to chlorophyll production. Potassium deficiency is seen first on the older, lower leaves. The leaves begin to yellow between the veins from the leaf tips and margins (leaf edge), and the edges begin to brown. Potassium toxicity is similar to phosphorus toxicity, but potassium toxicity results in root loss, therefore affecting a plant's ability to take up water and nutrients.

Sulfur is commonly added to the soil (a different formulation of sulfur is used as a fungicide) to lower pH over time. It encourages the production of chlorophyll (responsible for the green color in leaves). Sulfur deficiency occurs on new growth. The leaves and leaf veins turn yellow and the roses become stunted. Excessive sulfur causes the leaf veins to turn

yellow, followed by rapid loss of the lower leaves.

Zinc promotes water uptake. A deficiency appears as an interveinal chlorosis (yellowing between the veins), stunted growth, smaller foliage, thick stems, rosetting of new shoots and a whitish appearance. An excess of zinc reduces the uptake of manganese.

Ladybird beetle larva

Bonica

John Davis

Rosa glauca

Easy-to-grow Roses

groundcover roses
species roses
Ballerina
Belle Amour
Bonica
Buff Beauty
City of York
François Juranville
Gourmet Popcorn
Ingrid Bergman
Jens Munk
John Davis
Madame Hardy
Mountbatten
New Dawn
Nuits de Young
Queen Elizabeth
Sombreuil
Tournament of Roses
Tuscany Superb
Warm Welcome

Shade-tolerant Roses

Ballerina
Blanc Double de Coubert
Bonica
Buff Beauty
Charles de Mills
Felicia
Frau Dagmar Hastrup
Golden Wings
Hénri Martin
Heritage
Mutabilis
New Dawn
Rosa glauca
Sandalwood
Sweet Chariot

Drought-tolerant Roses

groundcover roses
Constance Spry
Eglantyne
Mary Rose
Roseraie de l'Haÿ
Stanwell Perpetual

Salt-tolerant Roses

pavement roses
rugosa roses
Barbra Streisand
Hansa
Sir Thomas Lipton

Disease-resistant Roses

groundcover roses
species roses
Alexander Mackenzie
Altissimo
Beauty Secret
Belle Amour
Blanc Double de Coubert
Bonica
City of York
Dortmund
Dublin Bay
Elina
Frau Dagmar Hastrup
Gerda Hnatyshyn
Hébé's Lip
Hénri Martin
Honor
Ispahan
Jens Munk
Morden Snowbeauty
Nuits de Young
Pat Austin
The Fairy
Winnipeg Parks
Warm Welcome

Constance Spry

Elina

Pat Austin

About This Guide

This book showcases 144 roses ideal for the Pacific Northwest, divided into nine sections: species, old garden, shrub, groundcover, climbers and ramblers, hybrid tea, floribunda, grandiflora and miniature. Each section begins with an explanation of the characteristics of the class. The roses are arranged alphabetically according to the name they are most commonly known by. Alternative names are given below the main heading.

Clearly displayed in each entry are the features of the rose: the flowers' color, size and scent; height and spread ranges; bloom seasons and hardiness zones (see map, p. 8). Each entry contains information pertinent to growing and enjoying the rose.

The introduction to the book has tips for buying, planting, growing and caring for roses. The Glossary of Pests & Diseases beginning on page 80 provides information on detecting and solving common problems.

Because our region is so climatically diverse, we refer to seasons only in a general sense. Keep in mind the timing and duration of seasons in your area when planning your rose garden. Hardiness zones, too, can vary within a region; consult a local rose society or garden center for specific information. The Resources section beginning on page 262 lists gardens, suppliers, soil-testing facilities and rose societies in the Pacific Northwest as well as books and websites about roses.

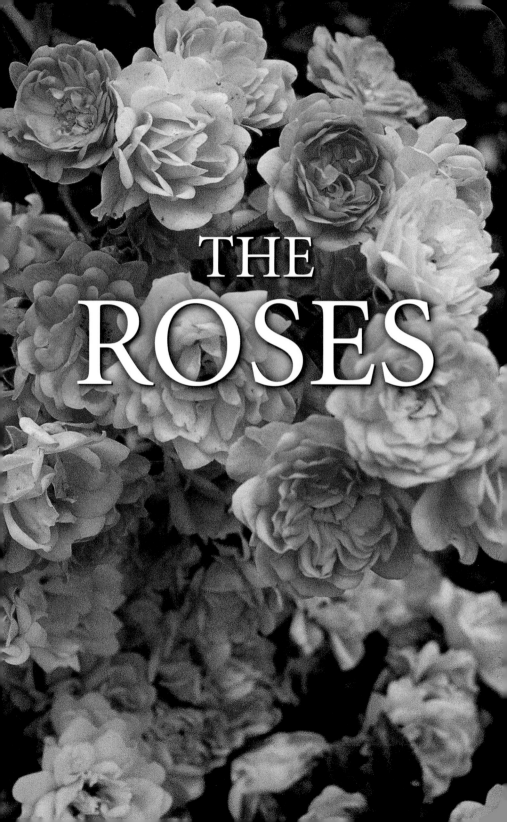

THE
ROSES

SPECIES ROSES

Species roses are roses that, when self-fertilized, produce seedlings that are identical to the parents. Species roses are very cold hardy and come in a variety of growth habits from vigorous climbers to compact shrubs. Use species roses in informal borders, woodland gardens or hedges.

Species roses usually flower once a year and produce attractive hips. Some species roses have excellent fall color. This group of roses tends to be more resistant to drought and disease compared to modern roses. Unfortunately, species roses are not widely available, but the results are well worth the search.

Rosa gallica officinalis

Other names:
Apothecary's Rose, Provins
Rose, Red Damask, Red
Rose of Lancaster, Maxima,
Officinal Rose, Crimson
Damask Rose, Rose of
Provins, *R. rubra*

Flower color:
deep pinkish red

Flower size: 3–3¹/₂"
(7.6–9 cm)

Scent: fresh and intense

Height: 4–5' (1.2–1.5 m)

Spread: 4–5' (1.2–1.5 m)

Blooms: mid- to late summer; no repeat blooming

Hardiness zones: 4–10

One of the oldest cultivated roses, *Rosa gallica officinalis* was brought from Damascus to France in the 13th century by Thibaut le Chansonnier. A painting of it from 1430 is on an altarpiece in the Ghent Cathedral. Preserves, syrups and powders that included traces of the rose were said to cure several ailments. Today this rose is notable for its culinary and medicinal value, its use in crafts and its ability to control erosion on steep sites.

✿ This species rose is a neat and bushy shrub with more bristles than thorns. It suckers freely—prune out unwanted suckers after the flowering cycle is complete. It blooms very early in the season and does not repeat. Small, rounded hips that turn reddish brown in fall immediately follow the flat, semi-double flowers on rough, dark foliage.

✿ Only general maintenance is required as this rose is highly disease resistant.

✿ The hips produce a large quantity of seed, so this rose naturally spreads and is suitable for naturalizing.

✿ Most descendants of the seven to eight species of wild roses derive from the group Gallicanae, which comprises *Rosa gallica* and its near relatives.

A candied form of the hips was used hundreds of years ago and is still considered a delicacy in Turkey.

Rosa glauca

This rose thrives where most plants could not survive. It is used by municipalities in open planting areas because it looks good and needs little care. The starry, pink blossoms make a striking contrast to the violet-tinted foliage. The foliage sometimes appears to change color depending on the degree of sun exposure. Clusters of small, rounded, dark red hips follow the flowers and remain on the shrub well into the following spring.

Other names: R. ferruginea, R. rubrifolia, Red-leafed Rose

Flower color: pink; white centers

Flower size: 1½" (3.8 cm)

Scent: little to none

Height: 6' (1.8 m); up to 12' (3.7 m) with support

Spread: 5–6' (1.5–1.8 m)

Blooms: early summer; no repeat blooming

Hardiness zones: 2–9

This rose received the Royal Horticultural Society Award of Garden Merit, the official stamp of approval from the experts. It is extremely popular among rosarians and novice gardeners alike.

✿ This species is sought by floral designers for the colorful, dainty foliage that is perfect for arrangements. It is equally beautiful in the garden. *Rosa glauca* is ideal for use as a hedge because of its vigorous nature and arching, thorny, purple stems. This rose has both looks and strength.

✿ *Rosa glauca* tolerates shade but prefers full sun, which improves the depth of the foliage color.

✿ Regular pruning will regulate the plant size and encourage new and colorful shoots.

✿ *Rosa glauca* was introduced into cultivation in Britain before 1830. Bushes can still be found on the terrace at the Crathes Castle in Aberdeen, Scotland.

Rosa Mundi

Other names:
R. gallica versicolor
Flower color: striped
white, pink and red
Flower size: 3–3½"
(7.6–9 cm)
Scent: strong
Height: 4½–5½'
(1.4–1.7 m)
Spread: 4–5' (1.2–1.5 m)
Blooms: mid-season;
no repeat blooming
Hardiness zones: 4–9

*This rose is known by
many names including*
R. gallica versicolor,
R. gallica *'Variegata,'*
R. gallica *'Versicolor,'*
Rosamund's Rose, Rose
of the World, R. x rosa
mundi, R. gallica rosa
mundi *'Weston,'*
R. gallica variegata
'Thory' and R. gallica
versicolor *'Linnaeus.'*

A sport of *Rosa gallica officinalis,* this rose discovered in the 16th century bears semi-double, striped, fragrant blossoms. The flowers are borne on upright stems with rough-textured, medium green foliage. Rosa Mundi is sometimes confused with *Rosa damascena* but is superior to that species. It is a compact, rambling, rounded shrub that boasts the most striking and earliest blooms of all the striped species roses. The blooms will often revert to a non-stripe, creating a blend of striped and solid flowers. No two flowers have the same striping pattern or degree of coloration. Roundish orange hips appear after the flowers have finished on canes with more bristles than thorns.

✿ Profuse flowering may cause the stems to become weighed down. Provide support or prune in spring so the shrub doesn't grow taller than 3–3½' (91–107 cm). Prune out the old wood and cut the new shoots down by one-third after flowering to maintain good air circulation and vigor. This rose can suffer dieback if temperatures drop below −13° F (−25° C).

✿ This species rose prefers well-mulched soil in an open site. It bears an abundance of healthy foliage impervious to most diseases. This rose excels on the coast and is very popular for its striking color and wonderful display of blossoms.

Rosa virginiana

No serious rose lover should be without *Rosa virginiana*. Its traditional form and reliable bloom make it a must for classical or cottage garden settings. It bears single pink flowers in one large profusion in early summer. The flowers are sometimes mottled or a slightly deeper pink and expose long stamens. The gently serrated, glossy leaves are made up of seven to nine leaflets each.

Other names: Glossy Rose, Virginiana Rose

Flower color: medium pink

Flower size: 2–2½" (5–6 cm)

Scent: strong

Height: 5–7' (1.5–2.1 m)

Spread: 3' (91 cm)

Blooms: no repeat blooming

Hardiness zones: 3–11

❁ The foliage changes from bright green to rich reds and yellows in fall. Bright red, shiny hips appear alongside the glowing fall foliage. The profusion of color is supported by reddish brown canes.

❁ The canes are often bristly with hooked thorns, making this species ideal as an impenetrable hedge. It is also attractive in mixed beds and borders or left as a specimen in a sunny location. It is a vigorous suckering rose, to the point of being almost invasive, so leave enough room for it to flourish.

A white form, Rosa virginiana 'Alba,' performs in a similar manner but tends to be a little less showy.

OLD GARDEN

O ld garden roses are those that were discovered or hybridized before 1867. Most bloom once during the growing season, producing a large quantity of fragrant flowers for a short time. Hybridizing in this class continued after 1867, but hybrids are still classified as old garden roses. This large and diverse class includes the following groups.

Gallica

Gallica roses are forms of *Rosa gallica*, often called the French Rose. It was the dominant rose from the 12th to the early 19th centuries but was in cultivation even longer. Many varieties and hybrids were discovered and propagated. These roses have upright, tidy to free-branching growth and intensely fragrant flowers that bloom once a year. The stems are moderately prickly, and fall foliage and hips are red. This hardy rose does not mind a little shade. Use gallicas in beds or borders, as hedges or specimens.

Damask

Hybrids of *Rosa damascena,* damask roses are prickly, open, sprawling shrubs with intensely fragrant flowers. They have been cultivated for centuries for attar of roses, an expensive perfume and cosmetic base. Like the gallicas, damask roses played a role in the heredity of modern roses. There are two groups of damasks. Summer damasks, derived from crosses of *Rosa gallica* with *Rosa phoenicea,* bloom once a year. Autumn damasks, derived from crosses of *Rosa gallica* and *Rosa moschata,* bloom twice a year. Use damask roses in a border or train on a support. This group is hardier than most other old garden roses.

William Lobb

Centifolia

Centifolias, also known as cabbage roses, are very hardy, open shrubs with good pest and disease resistance and prickly stems. They are taller and more robust than gallicas. They bloom profusely with large, full, intensely fragrant flowers once a season. 'Centifolia' means '100-leaved', referring here to the large number of tightly packed petals. Centifolias are derived from *Rosa centifolia,* likely a cross of an autumn damask and an alba cultivar. Use centifolia varieties in large borders or as specimens.

Moss

Moss roses began as sports of centifolia and damask roses. Balsam-scented, moss-like growth is produced on the flower buds, on the stems and sometimes on the foliage. The feel of the moss indicates the rose's origin—if a rose has supple, fern-like moss, it has been derived from a centifolia, while a rose with stiff, prickle-like moss has been derived from a damask. Moss roses are generally hardy to zone 6. They perform just as beautifully in colder regions and thrive from year to year with adequate winter protection and the right care and attention.

Alba

Alba roses are upright, graceful, free-branching shrubs with excellent pest and disease resistance, very good cold hardiness and good longevity. They are very low maintenance and bloom once a year with small clusters of small, intensely sweet flowers. Alba roses derive from a cross of *Rosa canina,* the dog rose, and *Rosa damascena,* the damask rose. They have been in cultivation since at least the time of the Roman Empire and were described by Pliny the Elder in his work *Historia Naturalis.* Alba roses are in the ancestry of many early hybrids. They are suitable for borders and beds, planted en masse or as specimens.

China

China roses are compact, mostly smooth-stemmed, erect shrubs with an open habit. They tolerate high humidity, heat and drought. China roses are derived largely from *Rosa chinensis*, cultivated in China for centuries. They are not cold hardy but are highly disease resistant. There are few true China roses remaining in commerce, as they have been replaced by newer cultivars that are hardier and, for some, more appealing. The flowers emit a fruity yet spicy fragrance that is refreshing but not overwhelming.

Portland

Portland roses are small, rounded, prickly shrubs with reasonable cold hardiness and a dislike of hot, humid climates. They are reliable repeat bloomers. Sometimes referred to as damask perpetuals, portlands derived from autumn damasks, gallicas and China roses. Their outstanding characteristics include a late flowering cycle and excellent red color. Hybridizers crossed the portlands with the ever-blooming China roses to produce the forerunners of the hybrid perpetuals. Use portland roses in the bed or border, or try them in a hedge.

Belle Amour

Bourbon

The first bourbon rose, *Rosa borboniana*, was discovered on the Isle of Bourbon (now Reunion Isle, a small island in the Indian Ocean) in 1819 as a naturally occurring hybrid of China and autumn damask roses. Nearly all 19th-century hybridizers used this hybrid, and hundreds of cultivars were produced, with many of the best still widely available in commerce today. Bourbon roses are open, upright, vigorous shrubs with large, quartered flowers. They are mildly prone to blackspot and possess a variable level of cold hardiness. Use them in a border or bed, or train them on a fence, pillar, veranda railing or obelisk.

Hybrid Perpetual

Hybrid perpetuals are upright to free-branching, vigorous, prickly shrubs requiring winter protection in zone 6 or colder. This group is prone to fungal diseases in areas where the summers are very hot. Hybrid perpetuals are not truly perpetual as they do not bloom continuously, but they do bloom recurrently. They have a strong flush of blooms in spring, sporadic blooms through summer and a flush of blooms again in fall. The limited flower color ranges from pink to red to deep maroon. The foliage is generally disease resistant but susceptible to blackspot. This class has bourbon, portland and China roses in its ancestry and has virtually reached the end of its development, having no new introductions for at least 50 years. One hundred years ago this class was the dominant class for cut flowers and gardens, especially in colder regions where the tea roses were not hardy.

They are uncommon in commerce and highly valued by collectors.

Hybrid Spinosissimas

These roses derived from *Rosa spinosissima* and are low-growing, suckering shrubs with fern-like foliage. They are very hardy and long-lived, flowering profusely once a year in spring. The flowers are primarily single blooms in white, yellow or pink tones. The canes are heavily prickled although some varieties have few prickles. Many natural variations and hybrids have been introduced, but few remain in commerce. This group has been extensively used in gardens for hundreds of years. Occasionally new cultivars are introduced.

Noisette

Noisette roses, also called Champney roses, are vigorous climbing or sprawling roses. The first was discovered in South Carolina by John Champney and given to a nurseryman in France whose name was used for the class. Noisette roses derived from a cross between the China rose Parson's Pink China and *Rosa moschata*. Most cultivars were introduced in the 19th century, with a few remaining today. These roses are not cold hardy, sustaining damage when the temperature falls below freezing. They flower profusely in flushes from spring to fall, with up to 100 flowers per cluster. The heavy blooms have a tendency to weigh down the leggy canes, so support may be required. It is thought that this group introduced yellow and orange into the modern climbers. Also available in this class are dwarf roses suitable as bedding plants.

China and Tea Roses

China roses and tea-scented China roses were collected by European explorers in the late 19th century. Tea roses are upright, smooth to lightly prickly bushes or climbers derived from *Rosa x odorata*, a cross of *Rosa gigantea* and *Rosa chinensis* bred in China long ago, and should not be confused with modern hybrid teas. The name refers to the fragrance, which resembles crushed tea leaves.

Hénri Martin

The flowers are large and well formed but lack substance and strong canes. The teas provided the flower form, repeat-flowering habit and spicy fragrance to the hybrid tea class. They also passed along their intolerance of the cold. Historically tea roses were used in warm regions such as the southern U.S., but the hybrid teas are now more popular.

The original China roses were most often dwarf. They produced loosely cupped blossoms that became darker in the sun and tended to shatter when fully open and spent. Today's China roses bloom almost continuously and bear smooth foliage and stems. Both China and tea roses are suitable for beds or borders.

Belle Amour

Other names: none

Flower color:
medium pink

Flower size: 3½" (9 cm)

Scent: spicy and pungent, myrrh

Height: 5–6' (1.5–1.8 m)

Spread: 3–4' (91–122 cm)

Blooms: early summer; no repeat blooming

Hardiness zones: 4–10

C lassified as an ancient damask rose, Belle Amour is extremely easy to grow even in the worst soil or environmental conditions. It bears small clusters of cushion-shaped, medium pink flowers. The flowers' fragrance resembles the scent of myrrh or aniseed. The symmetrical blooms look like camellias, exposing bright yellow stamens among the papery pink petals. The flowers are followed by a large crop of colorful, roundish hips well into winter. Coarse, gray-green foliage covers the moderately thorny canes from top to bottom.

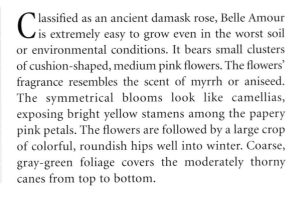

❀ Belle Amour is highly disease resistant and tolerates neglect.

❀ This upright, bushy rose was discovered in 1940 by an English woman, Nancy Lindsay, who found it at a convent in Elboeuf, Normandy. There is no record of who developed it or when. Some claim that Belle Amour is a cross between an alba and a damask. Graham Thomas, one of the most influential rosarians of our time, theorized that Belle Amour is a hybrid of Ayrshire Splendens, which has similar coloring and scent.

Old garden roses, with their delicate beauty, old-fashioned appearance and fantastic fragrance, are unique. Old garden roses are the ancestors of many of the roses found today.

Cardinal de Richelieu

Cardinal de Richelieu is easy to grow and bears an abundance of flowers accompanied by smooth, arching, burnished dark green stems. It has a lax, bushy and tidy growth habit and is extremely hardy. It bears fully double, dark red flowers that fade to royal purple and reveal a green button eye. The flowers then fade to slate gray as they age. The flower color is reminiscent of dark red grapes in a vineyard, at their peak and ready for harvest. The central petals are folded inward showing off a lighter tone on the reverse. The flowers are a complement to any mixed border or showy hedge.

❀ Cardinal de Richelieu is not a true gallica but is considered a triploid gallica-China hybrid. It produces the best flowers on the newest growth, and the flower color appears to change according to the light and time of day.

❀ Long-lasting, colorful flowers with long, smooth stems make Cardinal de Richelieu a wonderful rose for cutting. Cut the stems while still in bud to extend their vase life.

❀ Removing old and unproductive wood, feeding generously, providing fertile soil and practicing good cultivation will only increase the benefits offered by this shrub. Failing to prune moderately hard after flowering will cause the blooming to become more sporadic.

Other names: Cardinal Richelieu, Rose van Sian

Flower color: dark reddish purple

Flower size: 2½–3" (6–7.6 cm)

Scent: moderate, sweet, peppery

Height: 3–5' (91 cm –1.5 m)

Spread: 3–4' (91–122 cm)

Blooms: mid-summer; no repeat blooming

Hardiness zones: 4–9

This rose was developed in 1840 by Laffay in France and named after Cardinal de Richelieu, the chief minister to Louis XIII.

Charles de Mills

Other names: Bizarre Triomphant, Charles Mills, Charles Wills

Flower color: deep magenta pink

Flower size: 3½–5" (9–13 cm)

Scent: moderate to strong

Height: 4–5' (1.2–1.5 m)

Spread: 3–5' (91 cm–1.5 m)

Blooms: spring to early summer; no repeat blooming

Hardiness zones: 4–9

Charles de Mills is the largest rose in its family. It is often in garden books as the perfect example of an old garden rose. The unusually large, purply pink blooms pack 200 petals or more into each flower. The flower color can be violet, crimson, wine, purple or maroon. The flat-topped buds that open to flat blossoms, exposing a green button eye in the center, prove this to be a true gallica rose.

✿ The quartered blossoms are so full that the inner petals cluster and fold in toward the center. The petals look as if they have been clipped at the tips, resulting in puckered blooms, a very unusual form.

✿ Under ideal conditions this variety will become larger and bloom profusely. Its tolerance of poor soils and partial shade, however, makes it useful in just about any landscape setting, including mixed beds and hedging and as an exhibition rose. It is also suitable for wild gardens, alongside meadows or larger gardens.

✿ The best location would be where the fragrance can be fully enjoyed, near a bench or under a window.

✿ Very little maintenance is required to keep Charles de Mills looking great. Remove old and unproductive wood once flowering is complete to encourage dense, lush growth and heavier flowering.

This rose is a little prone to blackspot, so provide a location with adequate air circulation.

Duchesse de Montebello

This old garden rose is regarded as a gallica-damask hybrid by some, a China-gallica hybrid by others and a gallica-noisette hybrid by yet others, as the dispute about its origin continues. It bears double, loose clusters of globular flowers in soft pink, which is an unusual color for a gallica rose. The weight of the large, clustered, apple-scented flowers can cause the spreading, long, arching canes to droop.

✿ Matte grayish green foliage adorns the canes.
✿ With its spreading form, Duchesse de Montebello will need a little pruning to work well in a mixed bed or border.
✿ The foliage can become unsightly before a flush of new growth, so a little reshaping may be necessary once flowering is complete.

Other names: none
Flower color: soft pink
Flower size: 2½–3"
(6.3–7.6 cm)
Scent: strong, sweet, fruity
Height: 3–5'
(91 cm–1.5 m)
Spread: 4' (1.2 m)
Blooms: mid-season or later; no repeat blooming
Hardiness zones: 5–9

Jean Lannes, the Duc de Montebello, was one of Napoleon's marshals and close friends. This rose variety was named for his widow, grieving after her husband died in the Battle of Essling.

Fantin-Latour

Fantin-Latour, considered one of the most fragrant old garden roses, is officially classified as a centifolia but displays characteristics of other classes. It shares qualities with China and gallica roses, but not the repeat blooming. The flowers are produced in large clusters of flat, fully double, pale pink flowers, packed with 200 or more petals each. Each flower has a typical old rose button eye.

Other names: none
Flower color: pale pink
Flower size: 3–3½" (7.6–9 cm)
Scent: fresh, delicate and sweet
Height: 4–6' (1.2–1.8 m)
Spread: 4–5' (1.2–1.5 m)
Blooms: mid-summer; no repeat blooming
Hardiness zones: 5–9

❀ This rose bears smooth, matte foliage that doesn't seem to mind hot and dry weather. It tolerates poorer soils and needs to be pruned after flowering to promote prolific blooming the following year.

❀ This fragrant and showy rose is used frequently as a large spreading shrub. Once established, Fantin-Latour blends well into mixed beds and borders where space allows, and it is not troubled by larger tree roots. It grows even larger in cooler settings but can be pruned once the blooming is complete. When Fantin-Latour is supported and left unpruned, it can reach heights of 10' (3 m).

❀ Though centifolias are reputed to be prone to blackspot and to have unsightly flowers after rain, Fantin-Latour does not have these tendencies. This rose is moderately disease resistant but a little prone to mildew.

❀ It was named after the celebrated French painter Henri Fantin-Latour, known for his many still-life and old garden rose floral paintings.

Hébé's Lip

Hébé's Lip is regarded as a damask and sweetbriar cross. It produces fat, creamy white pointy buds covered in pinky red. The buds open into clusters of semi-double, white blossoms with showy gold stamens and a pinkish 'lip' or edge. Upright, stiff, prickly canes support heavily textured, dull, dark green foliage. The foliage has a strong apple fragrance most noticeable after a rainfall and in humid conditions.

✿ Do not prune until the flowering cycle is complete. Pruning at this time will not diminish any future flowering cycles because Hébé's Lip blooms best on old wood.

✿ This rose rarely experiences disease. It tolerates poor conditions and neglect so is ideal for those who have little time to tend their roses.

✿ This variety was discovered before 1846 in the U.K. by Lee and reintroduced in 1912 by Paul of the U.K.

Other names: Rubrotincta, Reine Blanche, Margined Hip

Flower color: white; pink edges

Flower size: 3" (7.6 cm)

Scent: strong, musky

Height: 3–5' (91 cm–1.5 m)

Spread: 4–5' (1.2–1.5 m)

Blooms: spring to early summer; no repeat blooming

Hardiness zones: 5–9

This tidy, compact and vigorous shrub was named after Hébé, the Greek goddess of youth, with the 'Lip' referring to the pink-edged petals.

Hénri Martin

Other names: Red Moss, Old Red Moss
Flower color: rich pinky red
Flower size: 3" (7.6 cm)
Scent: strong, sweet
Height: 3–5' (91 cm–1.5 m)
Spread: 4' (1.2 m)
Blooms: mid-summer; no repeat blooming
Hardiness zones: 4–9

This rose was introduced in France by Jean Laffay (1794–1852), who created and introduced nearly 40 roses and also created the hybrid perpetual class. This rose is widely known for its moss-covered stems and sepals that emit a subtle balsam scent. It bears clusters of rich crimson, fragrant blossoms that pale with age. The camellia-like rounded blossoms are semi-double to double and open flat. Profuse flowering happens only once, in the summer. It bears plentiful, disease-free, roughly textured foliage that looks fresh all season long.

❀ Support is required to prevent the arching, flexible canes from collapsing. Hénri Martin grows well on an obelisk, trellis, tripod or pergola.
❀ This rose is considered very healthy and tolerates light shade, hot and dry summers and poor soil. It may suffer a little winter dieback in colder regions. Prune out any deadwood in spring.
❀ This rose was named after Hénri Martin (1810–83), a famous French historian and writer.
❀ Usually considered a moss rose, Hénri Martin is sometimes regarded as a damask.

Once the flowers have finished, attractive orangy red hips begin to emerge, remaining on the shrub well into winter.

Ispahan

We know that this rose made its way from Persia to Europe by 1832, but no one knows for sure how old this rose is, although there are many theories. It bears long-lasting, double clusters of soft medium pink flowers with muddled centers. The beautiful flowers sit atop small, crisp, semi-glossy green leaves that form into a fairly dense, upright shrub. The stems have very few prickles.

Other names: Pompon des Princes, Rose d'Isfahan
Flower color: rich medium pink
Flower size: 2½–3" (6.3–7.6 cm)
Scent: intense, sweet
Height: 4–5' (1.2–1.5 m)
Spread: 3–4' (91–122 cm)
Blooms: mid-summer; no repeat blooming
Hardiness zones: 5–9

✿ Ispahan works well as hedging and in mixed borders, cutting gardens and planters.
✿ Exceptionally resistant to disease, this rose is only occasionally afflicted by powdery mildew.
✿ After it reaches maturity, prune after blooming by removing some of the oldest wood to prevent the plant from becoming unruly and out of control. The long canes can be pegged down or trained to trail along a fence.
✿ The vigorous flowering continues for over five weeks, making this one of the longest blooming of the once-blooming damask roses.

Ispahan was named after a city in Iran.

Jacques Cartier

Other names: Marchesa Boccella, Marquise Boçella, Marquise Boccella
Flower color: soft pink
Flower size: 4½–5" (11–13 cm)
Scent: rich and heady
Height: 3–4' (91–122 cm)
Spread: 24–36" (76–91 cm)
Blooms: summer to fall; repeat blooming
Hardiness zones: 5–9

Because there is no proof as to the breeder or location and date of origin for this rose, there is some debate that Jacques Cartier and Marchesa Boccella are the same rose. At rose shows, this variety is required to be known as Marchesa Boccella, but it is typically known throughout North America as Jacques Cartier. Classification varies as well—it is regarded as a hybrid perpetual, a damask or a portland rose.

❀ The blooms display a green button eye surrounded by soft pink, double, quartered rosettes. The flowers emerge among leathery, light green foliage that changes over time to blue-green. Typical of portland roses, the small flower clusters of this variety huddle on the shorter stems. The flowers are slightly obscured within the foliage—this tendency gives the plant a neat and tidy appearance but reduces the overall impact of the blooms.

❀ Jacques Cartier is highly disease resistant and easy to grow in containers, as hedging and in mixed beds and borders. It prefers fertile, well-mulched soil.

❀ It was named after the 16th-century French master navigator who explored the St. Lawrence River and searched for a Northwest Passage.

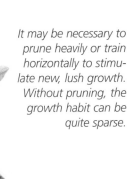

It may be necessary to prune heavily or train horizontally to stimulate new, lush growth. Without pruning, the growth habit can be quite sparse.

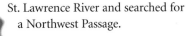

Madame Hardy

Give it everything it requires, and Madame Hardy will produce the most perfect white flowers you could ever imagine. This rose bears hundreds of large, flat, double, green-eyed, white blossoms. The emerging flowers sometimes display a hint of pale pink when they first open, and the blooms are set against densely packed, lush, matte green foliage. Each flower is made up of 150–200 petals that almost totally obscure the stamens.

❧ Once Madame Hardy is established, it is very easy to grow in mixed borders, beds and cut-flower gardens or as a specimen.

❧ Every three years or so prune the plant down to 1–2' (30–61 cm) just as the long shoots are beginning to get out of control. Remove the older wood down to the crown.

❧ This rose is extremely resistant to blackspot but highly susceptible to mildew. Hot sun immediately after a substantial rainfall can cause the leaves to develop small blotches.

❧ Madame Hardy tolerates poor soil conditions and light shade but tends to be less prolific under these conditions. It is best in full sun so the profuse flowering will be maintained for three to four weeks.

Other names: none
Flower color: white
Flower size: 3–3½"
(7.6–9 cm)
Scent: fresh and sweet with a hint of citrus
Height: 4–5' (1.2–1.5 m)
Spread: 3–5' (91 cm–1.5 m)
Blooms: mid-summer; no repeat blooming
Hardiness zones: 4–9

Since its 1832 introduction, Madame Hardy has been praised for its fragrance and received acclaim as the most beautiful white rose in the world. Alexandre Hardy, chief horticulturist of Paris' Luxembourg Castle, created this and many other rose varieties; he named this one after his beloved wife.

Mutabilis

Other names: Tipo
Idéale, *R. chinensis mutabilis,*
R. odorata 'Mutabilis,'
Butterfly Rose

Flower color: yellow,
then pink and crimson

Flower size: 2–3"
(5–7.6 cm)

Scent: little to none

Height: 4–6' (1.2–1.8 m)

Spread: 3–5'
(91 cm–1.5 m)

Blooms: mid-summer;
repeat blooming

Hardiness zones: 5–10

*The name is Latin for
'changing,' possibly
a reference to the
changing color of
the petals.*

Mutabilis flowers look like butterflies perched in among the leaves. This rose bears vermilion buds that open to buff yellow single flowers. The flowers then change into various shades of pink and finally evolve to a deep shade of crimson. It is common to see this flowering shrub in a state of constant change, similar to the color changes typical of wild China roses, from which this rose likely came. Each single flower is made up of an average of five velvety petals. The changing color palette is an unusual but desirable trait that would brighten even the gloomiest of sites.

❁ This variety has been known since 1896, but it was not introduced officially until 1932 when a Swiss botanist, Henri Correvon of Geneva, received it from Prince Ghilberto Borromeo's garden. No one knows where it originated or whether it had been naturally occurring.

❁ This rose could be used to climb up the side of a house, to cover outbuildings or as a large specimen. The size and shape will vary depending on the location. Some claim that this rose can reach heights of 10–25' (3–7.6 m) when left alone on a sturdy support.

❁ Soft red stems support the glossy, red-tinged dark green foliage, which is impervious to disease. This rose requires very little mainte-nance. It tolerates shade but is not fond of cold winds.

Nuits de Young

The name of this rose refers to Edward Young's 18th-century collection of poetry called *Night Thoughts*. It is an apt name for a rose with such dark blooms. The clusters of double, flat, dark purply maroon flowers, which reveal bright yellow stamens, sit atop dark red-brown, mossy, thorn-covered arching canes with small, dark, sparsely placed leaves. Its relatively short bloom period is not enough to detract from its many positive characteristics.

Other names: Old Black Rose, Old Black Moss
Flower color: dark maroon with purple
Flower size: 2½" (6.4 cm)
Scent: delicate, fruity
Height: 4–5' (1.2–1.5 m)
Spread: 3–4' (91–122 cm)
Blooms: mid-season; no repeat blooming
Hardiness zones: 4–9

✿ Nuits de Young looks great in mixed beds and borders or as a medium-sized specimen. It could also be planted in a staggered or straight row as a border or hedge.

✿ Its beauty and ease of care make Nuits de Young a rose any gardener can enjoy.

✿ This highly disease-resistant rose requires moist, well-drained and fertile soil.

✿ A light pruning may be necessary after flowering.

The classic flowers are meant to be celebrated as they emerge. With its unique and unfaltering beauty, it is simply a rose that shouldn't be taken for granted.

Reine des Violettes

The blooms of Reine des Violettes are close to a true blue. The flowers open carmine purple and turn violet mauve. The color is most striking later in the season, as the days become cooler and shorter. The abundant gray-green, smooth, peppery-scented foliage blends well with the color of the flowers. It is reminiscent of a gallica bloom in shape and color, but some say it more closely resembles a bourbon rose. It is classified as a hybrid perpetual.

Other names:
Queen of the Violets
Flower color: magenta with touch of lavender
Flower size: 3" (7.6 cm)
Scent: sweet, heady, peppery
Height: 3–5'
(91 cm–1.5 m)
Spread: 3–5'
(91 cm–1.5 m)
Blooms: early summer to fall; repeat blooming
Hardiness zones: 6–9

✿ This rose is somewhat susceptible to blackspot but more disease resistant than any other hybrid perpetual. Fungal problems are easily alleviated by proper watering practices (see Watering in the book's introduction).

✿ Reine des Violettes is a heavy feeder. Regular but careful pruning diminishes a leggy and sparse growth habit, and a hard pruning every three to four years will encourage a more solid form.

✿ Full sun, rich, well-drained soil and good air circulation are the only essentials for the success of this variety.

Reine des Violettes has an intoxicating fragrance.

Stanwell Perpetual

Stanwell Perpetual has an uncertain history. Some say that it was developed by one of the two—Lee and Kennedy—who marketed the rose in 1838. It was happened upon in a garden at Stanwell in England. When it was released, it was classified as a hybrid spinosissima. It is also known as a burnet cross. Regardless of the controversy and mystery, it can bear 100 or more blooms in one flush, completely obscuring the grayish green foliage. The quartered flowers have an average of 45–55 petals each. The color intensifies as the temperatures cool in late summer. The double flowers have muddled centers and frilled edges. The fragrant flowers are followed by only an occasional red hip. Each cane is well clothed in long, reddish prickles and light foliage touched with purple.

Other names: none
Flower color: pale pink, almost white
Flower size: 3–3½" (7.6–9 cm)
Scent: classic tea
Height: 3–5' (91 cm–1.5 m)
Spread: 4–6' (1.2–1.8 m)
Blooms: late spring to fall; repeat blooming
Hardiness zones: 3–9

✿ Pruning is unnecessary, but the floriferous growth is encouraged by removing old canes to the ground yearly. Don't be surprised to see this rose sucker. Prune out unruly growth when necessary.

✿ This beauty tolerates just about anything, including poor soil, drought, drenching rain, intense summers and hard winters. It is resistant to most disease but mildly prone to blackspot.

✿ Ideally suited to mass plantings in exposed areas and slopes, it is also stunning as a flowering border or impenetrable hedge.

The foliage emits a subtle, sweet aroma when wet with rain or morning dew.

Tuscany Superb

Other names: Double Velvet, Superb Tuscany, Superb Tuscan, Double Tuscany, Tuscany Supreme

Flower color: blackish mauve purple

Flower size: 3–4" (7.6–10 cm)

Scent: mild, sweet

Height: 4–5' (1.2–1.5 m)

Spread: 3–4' (91–122 cm)

Blooms: mid-summer; no repeat blooming

Hardiness zones: 4–9

Tuscany Superb originated in 1837 or earlier and is still receiving acclamations. It received the Royal Horticultural Society Award of Garden Merit of 1993.

Old garden roses are generally not very particular about what they need to grow well, and this one is no exception. Tuscany Superb is very easy to grow in just about any location, is impervious to disease and requires little to no pruning. Plant it where the fragrance can be enjoyed—near a bench, doorway or window.

✿ Rounded and compact, upright, neat and vigorous, Tuscany Superb is considered one of the most distinctive gallicas ever created. On the coast, it tends to sprawl and is easily trained along a fence or other support.

✿ Long bristly stems bear large, rough, dark green leaves and large clusters of blackish purple double flowers that obscure bright yellow stamens.

✿ Prune out the old and unproductive canes to encourage more compact growth and heavier flowering. It will sucker if the bud union is planted below soil level and even more profusely if grown on its own roots.

✿ This rose is resistant to blackspot but somewhat prone to mildew in the appropriate conditions once the flowering cycle is complete. It prefers an open site and grows very successfully in poor soil.

William Lobb

William Lobb is very popular and the most vigorous of all moss roses. The buds and sepals at the base of the flower clusters are covered in moss and smell of pine, especially when touched. Upright, arching, bristly canes form an open growth habit with coarse, large, dark gray-green leaves.

❀ The base is sparsely leafed, so plant another flowering shrub or perennial in front to disguise this characteristic.

❀ Hard pruning after flowering will create a more stout form while still showcasing the unique grayish brown moss and prickles. It can grow very large in zones 5 through 7. The long stems require support when climbing pillars, tripods, pergolas, walls, trellises, arbors and arches.

❀ This rose was bred by Laffay in France in 1855.

Other names: Duchesse d'Istrie, Old Velvet Moss
Flower color: dark crimson purple
Flower size: 3" (7.6 cm)
Scent: very sweet
Height: 6–8' (1.8–2.4 m)
Spread: 5–6' (1.5–1.8 m)
Blooms: mid-summer; no repeat blooming
Hardiness zones: 4–9

This rose was named after the plant huntsman who brought the Monkey Puzzle Tree from Chile and popularized it in England.

SHRUB

The category of shrub roses comprises a variety of rose groups. Shrub roses are easy to grow and generally very hardy. They can be compact or quite large and often have prickly stems. The newer varieties bloom continuously and have good pest and disease resistance. The following groups fall into this category.

English Roses

Roses in this small but expanding group were bred by David Austin Roses Ltd. and first became prominent in the 1970s. Although the flowers display the classic antiquity of old garden roses, they are modern roses and have the positive qualities of a newer generation, including improved disease resistance. The foliage is moderately prone to blackspot. They are specifically chosen for their

flower form, reliable growth habit, foliage and fragrance. They are ideal for cutting. The canes of English roses are not as robust as those of the hybrid teas, and often the large, beautiful flowers nod at the top of the canes. English roses generally need protection from cold winters.

Hybrid Musk Roses

Hybrid musks are a result of crossing *Rosa multiflora* with noisette varieties. Hybrid musks are very adaptable to climate. They do not mind the heat of the south and are hardy in all but the coldest parts of the Pacific Northwest. Protection during extremely cold winters is recommended. They are mostly recurrent bloomers and the flowers have a trademark musky tea scent.

Rugosas

This group contains a large number of varieties and hybrids of *Rosa rugosa*, a widespread, hardy rose with disease-resistant, wrinkled foliage. It is easy to identify hybrids that have *Rosa rugosa* as a parent. Rugosas are good, tough roses for the landscape, providing interest all year. They bloom in spring and fall, have attractive foliage and produce large orange-red hips that provide color through late fall and winter. They respond well to heavy pruning but should not be sprayed with any type of chemical, as the foliage is easily burned. They are suitable for beds, borders and hedges and as specimens. Because they tolerate salt, rugosas can be used near roads, sidewalks, pathways and driveways.

The Fairy

Vancouver Belle

Explorer Roses

Explorer roses were developed by crossing *Rosa rugosa* or *Rosa kordesii* roses for their strongest characteristics. Bred in L'Assomption, Quebec, and in Ottawa by Agriculture Canada, these roses can withstand temperatures as low as –40° F (–40° C), thriving from year to year with little to no care or winter protection. They are moderately to highly disease resistant and bear wonderful blooms, and most are repeat blooming. These roses are available in a range of colors and sizes, including climbers, and are most often found growing on their own roots. Although they were specifically bred for cold climates, they perform as beautifully in warmer regions.

Parkland Roses

This series is similar to the Explorer series as both series were bred from hardy, reliable rose stock. Parkland roses derive from *Rosa arkansana* crossed with floribunda and hybrid teas. They were bred specifically for the prairies at Agriculture Canada's Research Station in Morden, Manitoba. The result was a mix of hardy roses in beautiful colors, shapes and sizes. Generally the growth habit is compact and the blossoms are double to semi-double. Most roses in this series bloom repeatedly after the large flush of blooms in early summer and continue blooming until a hard fall frost. They bloom primarily on new wood and are grown on their own roots. Most of them produce hips.

Abraham Darby

Other names: Abraham, Country Abraham, Country Darby

Flower color: apricot yellow tinted with pink

Flower size: 4–5" (10–13 cm)

Scent: strong and fruity

Height: 5–6' (1.5–1.8 m)

Spread: 5' (1.5 m)

Blooms: early summer to late fall; repeat blooming

Hardiness zones: 5–9

When cut in bud, the long-lasting flowers are wonderful for arrangements.

Abraham Darby is one of the most widely grown roses developed by David Austin Roses Ltd., and justifiably so. It has a strong growth habit, fruity fragrance, reliable re-bloom and old-fashioned flowers. It is moderately disease resistant and extremely vigorous.

❀ This rose, named after one of the prominent figures of the Industrial Revolution, bears small clusters of large, double blooms on well-armed, arching stems with waxy, dark green leaves.

❀ Its flexible canes mean this rose can be trained as a climber. It is also ideal for borders or as a specimen when left in its natural form. Place it where the fragrance can be fully appreciated.

❀ Pruning is necessary only to remove dead or diseased wood and to help shape the bush into a well-formed, bushy, mounded shrub. It blooms well on new wood so can be pruned more if needed.

❀ Abraham Darby is not very resilient in a rainstorm because its weight makes it prone to collapse. It thrives in good weather and is only slightly prone to blackspot and rust.

Adelaide Hoodless

Adelaide Hoodless was one of the first Parkland roses to become available to the public and has remained popular ever since its 1973 introduction. It bears clusters of 35 or more semi-double, cupped flowers intermittently through the season. Glossy, dark green foliage is borne on arching stems that mature into a rounded form. A single plant can produce up to 100 flowers at one time.

✿ Deadheading is necessary during summer, but when fall approaches, the flowers should be left on the plant to allow the hips to form, signaling the shrub to begin preparing for winter.
✿ Pruning is required only to encourage a more prolific blooming cycle or to remove diseased or dead wood.
✿ Prevention to curtail blackspot may be necessary. Plant in a location that's open and airy and has good drainage. Water at the base in early morning.
✿ This rose was named after Adelaide Hoodless (1857–1910), a Canadian social reformer who founded the Women's Institute in 1897. The naming of the rose commemorated the institute's 75th anniversary.

Other names: none
Flower color: deep, dark red
Flower size: 3" (7.6 cm)
Scent: light
Height: 3–6' (91 cm–1.8 m)
Spread: 3–6' (91 cm–1.8 m)
Blooms: spring to fall; repeat blooming
Hardiness zones: 2–9

Adelaide Hoodless was one of the first truly hardy red roses made available to the public.

Alba Meidiland

Other names: Alba
Meillandecor, Alba
Sunblaze, Meidiland Alba
Flower color: white
Flower size: 1" (2.5 cm)
Scent: none
Height: 3–4'
(91–122 cm)
Spread: 3–6'
(91 cm–1.8 m)
Blooms: mid-season;
repeat blooming
Hardiness zones: 4–9

Alba Meidiland was originally bred in France in 1986, one of a series of low-maintenance, groundcover shrub roses developed for beautification beside highways. This rose has a vigorous, spreading growth habit and is extremely resistant to disease. It tolerates poor soil and neglect. Added to all these qualities is its ability to produce a profusion of long-lasting blooms all season.

✿ Alba Meidiland is a fantastic groundcover shrub
   suitable for any sunny location. It can also be
   used in mixed borders, in containers, on embankments to prevent erosion or as specimens or
   weeping standards.
✿ This rose bears large clusters of white flowers that
   develop a hint of pink with age. Each flower consists of 40 or more petals in a double, cupped form.
✿ The long-stemmed flowers are used for cutting
   and arrangements. Unfortunately the lovely flowers
   hold no scent at all, the only downfall of this tough
   rose contender.

Alexander Mackenzie

Alexander Mackenzie is known not only for its beauty and scent but also for its outstanding disease resistance. It bears fragrant double flowers in clusters of 6 to 12 on a tall, upright form. The glossy, light green foliage is lightly serrated, with hints of reddish purple on the stems. The long-lasting flowers resemble the blossoms of a hybrid tea or grandiflora rather than those of an Explorer.

❀ This rose is extremely hardy and vigorous and is highly resistant to mildew and blackspot. It requires very little maintenance; removing dead-wood in spring is the only pruning necessary.

❀ Deadheading regularly will encourage a longer, more prolific bloom cycle.

❀ Alexander Mackenzie is very hardy and can survive to zone 2b with some dieback, depending on the depth of any snow. It is one of the hardiest of the Explorer series. It deserves to be seen more often in climates and zones other than just cold winter climates.

Other names: A. Mackenzie, Alex Mackenzie

Flower color: deep red with hot pink

Flower size: 2½–3" (6–7.6 cm)

Scent: mild

Height: 5–7' (1.5–2.1 m)

Spread: 5–7' (1.5–2.1 m)

Blooms: spring to fall; repeat blooming

Hardiness zones: 3–9

Sir Alexander Mackenzie was a noted explorer and fur trader, and the first person to cross the North American continent and reach the Pacific Ocean.

Ballerina

Other names: none
Flower color: pinkish white; darker pink edges
Flower size: 1–2" (2.5–5 cm)
Scent: subtle musk or sweet pea
Height: 3–4' (91–122 cm)
Spread: 4' (1.2 m)
Blooms: mid-season; repeat blooming
Hardiness zones: 4–9

The flowers have been compared to apple blossoms, but this rose was given its name because the blooms resemble a ballerina's skirt.

B allerina was raised by Reverend Joseph Hardwick Pemberton and introduced by his gardener, John A. Bentall, in 1937. Reverend Pemberton was a distinguished English rosarian, exhibitor, president of the Royal National Rose Society and originator of the hybrid musk rose. After the reverend died, Bentall bred his own hybrid musk creations. Ballerina falls into several classifications including polyantha, hybrid musk and modern shrub. It bears large cascading clusters of single, dainty flowers. The lightly speckled flowers emerge a soft pink with a pale reverse and well-defined pink edges. The pink fades to a pinkish white eye at the base of the petals surrounding the golden stamens.

✿ The flowers are supported by a dense mass of small, semi-glossy leaves on almost thornless stems. Tiny orange-red hips follow the flowers in fall.
✿ Ballerina is relatively trouble free and resistant to most disease. It tolerates light shade and poor soil. The flowers may need deadheading after the first flush to keep the plant from looking tired.
✿ With its arching growth habit, this rose could work as a weeping standard. It is suitable for hedging, mixed borders, containers and mass groupings. It can also be trained as a climber on a trellis or fence.

Blanc Double de Coubert

Every rose garden should include one of these magnificent rugosas. Admittedly I am easily dazzled by white roses, but this 110-year-old rose has history and an outstanding reputation too. Coubert is the French village where its creator lived. It was introduced in 1892 in its home country. It bears leathery, wrinkled, dark green leaves. Loose-petaled, semi-double clusters of white, fragrant flowers are borne from buds occasionally flushed with a hint of pink. Each flower is made up of an average of 15–25 petals.

✿ Moderately vigorous, this arching, dense shrub tolerates light shade and most soils. It is highly resistant to disease.

✿ Unfortunately the soft-textured petals are easily marked and affected by rain, so they might appear spent not long after opening.

✿ Deadheading after the first flush will encourage more blooms. Stop deadheading closer to fall so hips will develop. The hips transform into reddish orange spheres that stand out among the stunning fall foliage.

✿ Blanc Double de Coubert is excellent for hedging, borders or specimens. The blossoms are ideal for cutting, but cut the stems when they are still partially closed to extend the flowers' vase life.

Other names: Blanc Double de Coubert, Blanc de Coubert
Flower color: crisp white with yellow stamens
Flower size: 3" (7.6 cm)
Scent: strong and sweet
Height: 5–7' (1.5–2.1 m)
Spread: 4–5' (1.2–1.5 m)
Blooms: spring to fall; repeat blooming
Hardiness zones: 3–9

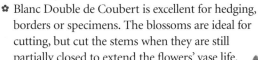

Bonica

Other names: Bonica '82, Meidomonac, Demon, Bonica Meidiland
Flower color: medium pink
Flower size: 1–2" (2.5–5 cm)
Scent: sweet and delicate
Height: 3–5' (91 cm–1.5 m)
Spread: 3–4' (91–122 cm)
Blooms: summer to fall; repeat blooming
Hardiness zones: 4–9

A Meilland introduction in 1982, Bonica was the first modern shrub rose to be named an All-America Selection when it received that honor in 1987. It is durable and highly recommended for mixed beds, containers, hedges, cut-flower gardens or as a groundcover, standard or specimen. It bears an abundance of semi-glossy, rich foliage, beautiful enough to stand on its own. The blooms are lightly scented. Bright orange hips follow the double pink rosettes through winter.

✿ Easy to maintain, this rose tolerates most conditions including shade and poor soils and is disease resistant and hardy.

✿ Bonica is a tidy sprawling rose of modest size that blooms profusely through most of the growing season. It is suitable for just about any type of location.

It's not surprising that this beautiful rose has been popular throughout the world since its introduction.

Buff Beauty

O ver the years there has been a little controversy regarding the parentage and breeder of Buff Beauty. Some claim that Pemberton developed this hybrid musk in 1922. Others say that Bentall or his widow created it in 1939. Regardless, this variety is not only useful but beautiful as well. It bears sprays of small, double, apricot yellow flowers. The colorful blooms contrast beautifully with the coppery plum foliage that matures to a deep, dark green. The flowers fade to a creamy buff over time.

Other names: none

Flower color: rich apricot yellow

Flower size: 3" (7.6 cm)

Scent: sweet tea, tropical fruit, musk

Height: 5–6' (1.5–1.8 m)

Spread: 5–6' (1.5–1.8 m)

Blooms: mid-season; repeat blooming

Hardiness zones: 4–9

✿ Buff Beauty tolerates less fertile soils and partial shade. It withstands poor weather and continues to bloom profusely until fall.

✿ The long stems make this a good choice for a cutting rose. It is also suitable for hedging when plants are placed close together. It can be trained as a small climber on low fences and pillars.

✿ Buff Beauty is striking when mixed with a variety of colorful plants or left alone to show off in its own container.

✿ This rose is vigorous and dense, exhibits a spreading tendency, yet is strong and self-supporting. It will perform with very little to no care.

With its unique flower color and handsome foliage, this rose is almost a collectible, ideal for the rose enthusiast.

Cuthbert Grant

Other names: none

Flower color:
dark, crimson red

Flower size: 4" (10 cm)

Scent: strong

Height: 3–4'
(91–122 cm)

Spread: 3–4'
(91–122 cm)

Blooms: early summer
to fall; repeat blooming

Hardiness zone: 3

Three years after its introduction, Cuthbert Grant received the Award of Merit from the Western Canadian Society for horticulture. It was also chosen as the centennial rose for the province of Manitoba, Canada, in 1970.

Cuthbert Grant is at different times considered a member of the Parkland series, a suffulta hybrid or a modern shrub rose. Regardless of its classification, this rose deserves to be used more. It is cold hardy but displays the same great characteristics in warmer zones, too. It offers so much—prolific blooming, excellent disease resistance and vigor. Oval buds open into large, velvety, semi-double clusters of cupped flowers.

✿ The rich-looking flowers are intensely fragrant and worthy of any garden setting. The blooms are accompanied by glossy, disease-resistant foliage produced on upright, vigorous stems.

✿ The process of deadheading is slightly different for this rose. Remove the entire cluster of flowers as they fade, rather than a single flower at a time. Remove any deadwood in spring. New vigorous shoots will emerge.

✿ Cuthbert Grant led his people to victory at Seven Oaks in Manitoba in 1816.

Eglantyne

Eglantyne reminds me of roses depicted in classic oil paintings created hundreds of years ago. Though it looks old fashioned, it was introduced in 1994 by David Austin Roses Ltd. With its exquisite form, it is considered by its creator to be one of his most beautiful hybrids. It bears fully double pale pink rosettes, and the blossoms are very large and cupped. Most of the petals have gently ruffled petals that turn up at the edges, forming a shallow saucer filled with an abundance of tiny petals. Attractive and healthy foliage covers the tall upright stems.

Other names: Eglantine, Eglantyne Jebb
Flower color: light pink
Flower size: 3–4" (7.6–10 cm)
Scent: true rose, sweet and strong
Height: 4–6' (1.2–1.8 m)
Spread: 3' (91 cm)
Blooms: late spring to early fall; repeat blooming
Hardiness zones: 5–9

❀ Eglantyne's bushy and perfect growth habit makes it ideal among lower-growing material, whether woody or herbaceous. It is exquisite when flowering, but when not blooming it can sometimes be lost among too many plants. Place it where adjacent plant material will not overwhelm it.

❀ Considered a very healthy rose, Eglantyne is only mildly prone to blackspot and tolerates drought.

❀ English roses generally require very little to no pruning and are a delight to grow. In warmer climates, long shoots that seem out of place could emerge. These shoots need to be pruned out to encourage balanced growth.

❀ Eglantyne was named after Eglantyne Jebb, who founded the Save the Children charity fund during World War I.

Though their names are similar, Eglantyne should not be confused with the species rose R. eglanteria.

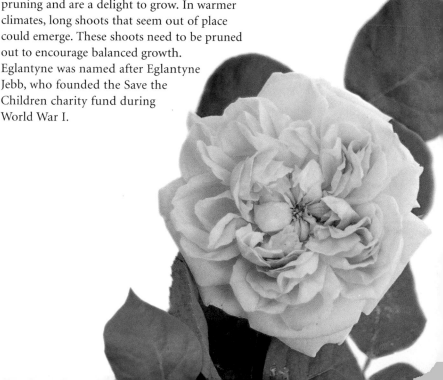

Felicia

Other names: none
Flower color:
blush peach
Flower size: 2–3"
(5–7.6 cm)
Scent: sweet and
fairly strong
Height: 5' (1.5 m)
Spread: 5' (1.5 m)
Blooms: summer to fall;
repeat blooming
Hardiness zones: 4–9

*Felicia makes a
spectacular cluster-
flowered shrub when
pruned hard in early
spring. Lighter pruning
creates a symmetrical
specimen.*

Felicia bears a profuse show of apricot buds that open to a blush peach. The flowers pale to off white as they age, more frequently in spring and fall. This rose blooms sporadically throughout summer and produces mounds of glossy foliage among large panicles of long-lasting flowers well into late fall.

✿ Felicia is suitable for cutting, hedging, containers and mixed borders and beds. It is best suited to partial shade and is highly resistant to disease.
✿ Felicia requires deadheading to promote further blooming, but do leave some flowers on the plant so hips will develop at the end of the growing season. The late hips will also signal the plant that winter is just around the corner. Eventually the hips turn shades of deep red and remain on the shrub until the following spring.
✿ This rose is considered one of the best of its class. It won the National Rose Society Certificate of Merit in 1927 and the Royal Horticultural Society Award of Garden Merit in 1993.

Flower Carpet

Flower Carpet was developed in 1991 and claimed to offer 'flowers for 10 months' and 'total disease resistance.' The claims proved a little too optimistic, but this variety is still beautiful and multi-faceted. Vigorous, shiny, plentiful foliage complements the double, hot pink flowers. The blooms are borne in large clusters with bright yellow stamens, creating a dense, colorful carpet of flowers, hence the name.

✿ A characteristic of its rambler parentage is that the prolific flowering begins a little later than for most roses, and at times there are no blooms at all. A hard early spring prune every couple of years will restore the vigor of any Flower Carpet plant that has become too woody. Cut it down to 10–12" (25–30 cm) above ground at that time, removing any old wood.

✿ Deadheading isn't really necessary because the hips are so small that they do not inhibit blooming. The petals drop cleanly in cool weather but cling in warmer temperatures.

✿ Flower Carpet can be used as a groundcover for a sunny location or as a low hedge. It can also be used in containers, mixed borders or beds. It is frequently integrated into golf course landscapes and along highways and commercial properties.

✿ This rose's disease resistance is reliable, but blackspot may occur in wetter climates and powdery mildew in drier conditions.

✿ A new color of Flower Carpet has been introduced almost every year since its original release, including white and a variety of pink shades. Watch for Appleblossom, White, Pink, Red and Coral, the color introduced in 2002.

Other names:
Heidetraum, Noatraum, Emera, Blooming Carpet, Emera Pavement, Pink Flower Carpet

Flower color:
deep hot pink

Flower size: 2" (5 cm)

Scent: little to none

Height: 30–36" (76–91 cm)

Spread: 3–4' (91–122 cm)

Blooms: summer to early winter; repeat blooming

Hardiness zones: 4–9

Flower Carpet is popular and easy to grow for either the beginner or the expert.

Frau Dagmar Hastrup

Other names: Frau
Dagmar Hartopp
Flower color:
light silvery pink
Flower size: 3½–4"
(9–10 cm)
Scent: strong
cinnamon and cloves
Height: 3–4'
(91–122 cm)
Spread: 4' (1.2 m)
Blooms: spring to fall;
repeat blooming
Hardiness zones: 2–9

*Bees love this rose.
If you want to attract
bees to a sunny
vegetable garden,
then plant this rose
nearby.*

Frau Dagmar Hastrup is one of the most compact-growing rugosas, ideal for a smaller garden. It is sturdy and vigorous with a spreading habit and strong disease resistance. Pale, silvery pink, shallow-cupped flowers are followed by huge, tomato-shaped, dark red hips. Wrinkled leathery foliage covers the prickly gray canes.

✿ Frau Dagmar Hastrup is used widely in natural woodland settings, shrub borders, low ground-cover hedges or in front of larger-growing species roses or flowering shrubs.
✿ This low-maintenance rose tolerates a little shade to full exposure.
✿ This variety is highly resistant to disease but may experience dieback in harsh winters. It will reshoot.
✿ A small thicket of stocky suckers will form when the bud union is planted below ground level. Make sure you plant it at the correct level.
✿ The foliage changes from maroon to deep russet gold in fall. Along with the showy hips, this rose adds outstanding color to a fall setting when everything else is about to finish.
✿ Frau Dagmar Hastrup was originally released as a 1914 introduction from Denmark. It won the Royal Horticultural Society Award of Garden Merit in 1993.

Golden Wings

Golden Wings has set the standard for single-flowered yellow shrub roses since its 1956 introduction. It is a living memorial of its creator, Roy Shepherd, a famous rosarian who died in 1962. It bears delicately ruffled, soft yellow flowers that emerge long before almost any other rose and bloom continuously throughout the season. The cupped flowers consist of an average of five to seven petals that open into large saucers with prominent amber stamens. Each cluster is followed in fall by uniquely shaped green hips. It vigorously produces the strong, prickly stems covered with clear, light green leaves.

Other names: none

Flower color: medium yellow

Flower size: 4–5" (10–13 cm)

Scent: subtle orange and honey

Height: 4½–5½' (1.4–1.7 m)

Spread: 4½' (1.4 m)

Blooms: summer to fall; repeat blooming

Hardiness zones: 4–9

✿ Deadhead to extend the blooming season. It is best to prune Golden Wings back pretty hard to reduce the possibility of straggly growth.

✿ This rose tolerates poor or less-fertile soils and partial shade. The foliage is highly disease resistant but more prone to blackspot along the coast.

✿ Use this variety in mixed borders or hedges. It is considered one of the most valuable landscape roses available. It can provide structure within a wide border and is very effective as a specimen when left alone.

✿ Without adequate winter protection in colder areas, this variety may experience severe dieback, or die completely.

Graham Thomas

Other names: English
Yellow, Graham Stuart
Thomas

Flower color:
deep butter yellow

Flower size: 4–5"
(10–13 cm)

Scent: strong,
old-fashioned tea

Height: 5–7' (1.5–2.1 m)

Spread: 5' (1.5 m)

Blooms: early summer
to fall; repeat blooming

Hardiness zones: 5b–9

Graham Thomas was developed in 1983 by David Austin Roses Ltd. and was the first true yellow English rose. It was named after one of the most influential rosarians of our time. It bears beautiful apricot-pink buds that open into large golden yellow blooms. The double blooms carry up to 35 petals and fade gracefully in time. The flowers remain cupped until the petals fall cleanly from the plant. This rose is very dense and upright in form, bearing an abundance of light green leaves.

✿ In warmer climates this extremely vigorous rose
  will grow taller if supported, developing into a
  pillar style or climbing rose. A light pruning will
  allow Graham Thomas to remain a little smaller
  if desired, but this may naturally occur in cooler
  climates.
✿ Long, flexible stems often flop under the
  weight of the beautiful but short-lived flowers.
✿ Deadheading may be required to extend the
  prolific blooming cycle.
✿ Wet weather will not trouble this rose, but excessive heat may cause reduced flowering, problems
  with mildew and fading flower color.
✿ Graham Thomas received the Royal Horticultural
  Society Award of Garden Merit in 1993.

*Its narrow, upright growth
habit makes this rose useful
as a standard or towards
the back of a mixed border.*

Hansa

H ansa, first introduced in 1905, is one of the most durable, long-lived and versatile roses. It's not unheard of to come across buildings that have been abandoned for decades and find Hansa specimens blooming. It bears deeply veined, leathery foliage on arching, thorny canes. Large, double, loose clusters of dark mauve-red blooms make this rose showy enough for mixed borders and beds, hedges or specimens. Spectacular foliage and large, orange-red hips follow in fall.

✿ Canes five years and older may need to be pruned out to improve the vigorous flower production, which will naturally decline with age.

✿ This rose thrives in silty clay to sandy soils, freezing weather, salt air and wind. It tolerates hard pruning and poor conditions but dislikes alkaline soils.

✿ In milder climates the plant might become leggy and the flower color may fade. Pruning regularly can correct the growth habit.

Other names: Hansen's
Flower color: mauve purple
Flower size: 3–3½" (7.6–9 cm)
Scent: strong, cloves
Height: 4–7' (1.2–2.1 m)
Spread: 5–6' (1.5–1.8 m)
Blooms: summer to fall; repeat blooming
Hardiness zones: 3–9

Like most rugosas, Hansa tolerates neglect while still profusely flowering throughout the season.

Henry Hudson

Other names: none
Flower color: white
Flower size: 3" (7.6 cm)
Scent: intense, cloves
Height: 24–36" (61–91 cm)
Spread: 24"–4' (61–122 cm)
Blooms: spring to fall; repeat blooming
Hardiness zones: 2–9

Henry Hudson was introduced in 1976 and has lived up to its claims of being easy to maintain, hardy and resistant to mildew and blackspot. This semi-dwarf, rounded shrub produces pink-tinged buds that open to white, semi-double, flat flowers that showcase the golden stamens. The flowers are reminiscent of double apple blossoms. It is known to bloom profusely from the moment a bud emerges in spring well into fall. Hips do not follow the spent flowers.

✿ Dense, wrinkly, dark green leaves are typical of its rugosa parentage. Rugosas have foliage that can become marked, mottled or burned if sprayed with pesticides.
✿ With its compact, thorny, impenetrable growth, this rose is suitable for use as a low hedge, barrier or groundcover or in a mixed bed or border.
✿ This rose tolerates a little more shade than other Explorer roses. The finished flowers don't fall cleanly from the plant for long periods, so deadhead to keep the plant tidy and extend the bloom cycle. Pruning is not necessary.

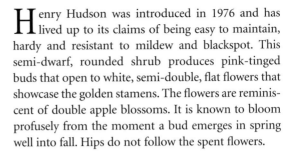

Henry Hudson was the first European explorer to sail into Hudson Bay, in 1610. His name lives on not only in a rose, but also a bay, a river and a strait, none of which was discovered by him. Hudson died while trying to find the Northwest Passage. He, his son and seven of his crew were sent adrift by mutineers and were never seen again.

Henry Kelsey

Henry Kelsey is one of the more unusual Explorer roses. It is larger and can be trained as a climber or left as an arching, pendulous specimen. Intense red blossoms are borne in heavy clusters of 18–20 fully double cupped blooms with reflexed petals and bright gold stamens. The blossoms fade shortly before falling from the shrub. Thorny stems support glossy, dark foliage that is sometimes affected by blackspot but is highly resistant to powdery mildew and rust. It is ideal for just about any climate.

Other names: none
Flower color: bright red
Flower size: 2½–3" (6.3–7.6 cm)
Scent: sharp and spicy
Height: 6–8' (1.8–2.4 m)
Spread: 6' (1.8 m)
Blooms: summer to fall; repeat blooming
Hardiness zones: 2–9

✿ Henry Kelsey takes a couple of years to reach its full potential, but it is well worth the wait. It will begin to bloom profusely one to two years after planting. Guaranteed, Henry Kelsey will produce an abundance of lush growth among hundreds of blooms when given the chance.

✿ Henry Kelsey is most often trained as a climber, but if you want to use it as a shrub, prune hard after the flowering cycle is complete. Pruning may be necessary to remove the older canes and deadwood as well.

✿ During a severe winter with little or no snow, it may completely die back. It will produce new shoots and will bloom for a shorter time the following year.

This rose was named after a British explorer who extended the trade routes of the Hudson's Bay Company.

Heritage

Other names: Roberta
Flower color: pale blush pink
Flower size: 4–5" (10–13 cm)
Scent: sweet with lemon undertones
Height: 5–6' (1.5–1.8 m)
Spread: 4–5' (1.2–1.5 m)
Blooms: summer to fall; repeat blooming
Hardiness zones: 4–9

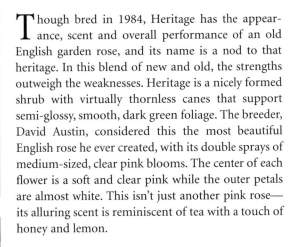

Though bred in 1984, Heritage has the appearance, scent and overall performance of an old English garden rose, and its name is a nod to that heritage. In this blend of new and old, the strengths outweigh the weaknesses. Heritage is a nicely formed shrub with virtually thornless canes that support semi-glossy, smooth, dark green foliage. The breeder, David Austin, considered this the most beautiful English rose he ever created, with its double sprays of medium-sized, clear pink blooms. The center of each flower is a soft and clear pink while the outer petals are almost white. This isn't just another pink rose—its alluring scent is reminiscent of tea with a touch of honey and lemon.

✿ Heritage performs best in fertile, well-mulched soil in mixed borders, hedges and beds.

✿ The graceful flowers do not lend themselves to cutting and are better left to adorn the garden instead of your house. The flowers are very short-lived and fragile, though easily replaced.

✿ This rose is moderately resistant to disease; take the proper measures to prevent mildew and blackspot, including watering at the base rather than from overhead. It is prone to foliage burn, so partial shade is recommended.

Some rose growers have said that Heritage blooms in sparse and sporadic waves when young, but we've experienced profuse blooming and overall vigorous growth in the first year. The blooming only increases over time, resulting in a prolific flowering shrub suitable for any garden setting.

Hope for Humanity

Hope for Humanity is a small, compact, very low-growing rose with an open growth habit. Pointed buds emerge in mid-summer. The flowers open into double, cup-shaped, deep red flowers that resemble the blooms of high-centered hybrid teas. The flower color is even more intense and deeper than that of another red Parkland rose, Cuthbert Grant (p. 134). The stunning red flowers are borne on strong, moderately thorny canes and continue to produce over a period of 10 to 14 weeks. The flowers emerge from overwintered buds, and continue to emerge on the current season's growth. Two to 15 flowers can make up one single cluster. A small white spot is on the inner base of many of the petals, and the outer side of each petal has a white and yellow spot. The blooms' subtle fragrance is sweet.

Other names: none
Flower color: blood red
Flower size: 3" (7.6 cm)
Scent: light
Height: 3' (91 cm)
Spread: 24" (61 cm)
Blooms: mid-summer to fall; everblooming
Hardiness zones: 3–8

✿ Hope for Humanity in an everblooming rose, not a repeat bloomer. It doesn't send out just one short-lived flush of blooms but blooms continuously and profusely for months.

✿ This low-maintenance rose may require a little care to prevent blackspot but is highly resistant to mildew and rust.

Introduced in 1995, Hope for Humanity was named in honor of the 100th anniversary of The Canadian Red Cross Society. The society had exclusive rights to the rose until 1998, when it became available for sale to the general public. It has been very popular ever since.

J.P. Connell

Other names: none
Flower color:
medium yellow
Flower size: 3–3½"
(7.6–9 cm)
Scent: strong, tea
Height: 5' (1.5 m)
Spread: 3–5'
(91 cm–1.5 m)
Blooms: summer to fall;
repeat blooming
Hardiness zone: 3–8

This rose may require a little patience because it can take a little longer to establish than other Explorer varieties. One- to two-year-old plants may flower sparsely and sporadically, but after its first two years this rose blooms profusely through most of the season. It bears high-centered, soft yellow flowers in early summer. The flowers resemble hybrid tea blossoms rather than the typical form of a hardier rose. The blooms are produced singly or in clusters of three to eight flowers. The flower color fades to a creamy pale yellow just before the bloom is finished. Medium green, glossy foliage contrasts well with the flowers on almost thornless stems.

❀ This tough and versatile rose is used frequently in mixed beds and borders or as a specimen in a smaller location. It is highly resistant to powdery mildew but somewhat prone to blackspot.

❀ J.P. Connell is prone to winter damage in hardiness zones colder than zone 3. Minimize damage by protecting the base with a thick layer of snow or mulch. Prune out the dead branches in spring to help the bush bear a flush of new growth.

❀ The first rose in the Explorer series that was not named after an explorer, this rose was named after a retired civil servant who had served as deputy minister of Agriculture Canada.

J.P. Connell was developed in 1987 and is the only yellow-blooming rose of the Explorer series.

Jens Munk

I first heard Jens Munk described as thornless— boy, did the source of that information turn out to be unreliable! After I pruned and deadheaded a large group of these roses, it must have taken me three days to remove the prickles from my fingers. Its overall beauty and spicy fragrance drew me in that day, and I've come to appreciate this rose over the years for its positive attributes.

Other names: none

Flower color: medium pink and purple

Flower size: 3" (7.6 cm)

Scent: spicy, mild

Height: 5–7' (1.5–2.1 m)

Spread: 4–5' (1.2–1.5 m)

Blooms: summer to fall; repeat blooming

Hardiness zones: 3–9

✿ Jens Munk vigorously grows into a rounded, dense shrub. It has a sprawling and unshapely form when young but evens out with maturity. This rose is extremely tough, highly disease resistant and drought tolerant. It requires very little to no maintenance.

✿ It bears prickly stems and wrinkly, shiny foliage that changes into a beautiful yellowy orange in the fall. Semi-double flowers are borne in pale pink clusters. Each petal is lightly streaked with white at the base and surrounds bright yellow stamens. Bright red hips follow the flowers in fall.

✿ With its vast number of prickles, Jens Munk makes an impenetrable medium-sized hedge. It blends beautifully into mixed beds and borders or works well when left as a specimen.

✿ Although Jens Munk is typically resistant to disease, it does have the foliage typical of rugosas. Do not spray the foliage with any pesticides. If there is a hint of mildew, remove and destroy the infected foliage rather than spraying.

This rose was named after a 17th-century Norwegian explorer.

John Cabot

Other names: none

Flower color: deep, vivid, reddish pink

Flower size: 2–3" (5–7.6 cm)

Scent: strong

Height: 8–10' (2.4–3 m)

Spread: 5–6' (1.5–1.8 m)

Blooms: early summer to fall; repeat blooming

Hardiness zones: 3–9

This rose was named after the first European since the Vikings to explore the mainland of North America and search for the Northwest Passage.

John Cabot was introduced in 1978 as the first climber in the Explorer series. It is vigorous and tough, requiring little to no maintenance. It is one of the best of the series, exhibiting semi-double clusters of blooms that lose their intense color over time. The prominent yellow stamens stand out among the cupped petals and light green foliage. The flower color can range from deep pink to reddish purple. Clusters of flowers emerge in summer and then bloom again sporadically from late summer to early fall.

❖ This variety is best trained as a climber but can be pruned into a smaller specimen once it has finished flowering. Train the branches to climb on a decorative support such as pergola, archway, trellis or obelisk.

❖ Pruning may be necessary to remove tip dieback in spring. Stems exposed during winter are vulnerable to seasonal damage, but pruning will help flowers develop on new shoots. This rose is highly resistant to disease.

❖ John Cabot has a reliable reputation backed up by a 1985 Certificate of Excellence from Britain's Royal National Rose Society.

John Davis

John Davis isn't just another pink rose. Its red buds open to large, double, pink flowers with a touch of creamy yellow at the base of each petal. The spice-scented clusters can consist of up to 17 flowers each. Long, graceful, arching red canes produce dark, glossy, tough foliage. This 1986 introduction has a trailing growth habit, unusual for an Explorer rose, and it is one of the longest blooming of the Explorer series.

Other names: none
Flower color: medium pink
Flower size: 3–3½" (7.6–9 cm)
Scent: strong, spicy
Height: 6–8' (1.8–2.4 m)
Spread: 6' (1.8 m)
Blooms: spring to fall; repeat blooming
Hardiness zones: 2b–9

This rose was named after an explorer from the 16th century who wrote a book about his final sailing voyage called the Traverse Book, *which became the model for present-day shipping log books.*

❀ John Davis is ideal as a windbreak or specimen or in a mixed shrub border or an exposed area where nothing else thrives. It is most often trained as a climber, and few other climbing roses have all the positive qualities this rose possesses. It is striking when trained on a charming wooden fence or support.

❀ This rose requires little to no maintenance, has healthy foliage and blooms profusely. It has a vigorous, strong and healthy growth habit. Pruning is unnecessary, but the leaves may need a little care to prevent blackspot and mildew—water early in the morning and water at the base rather than from above.

❀ This plant is sometimes targeted by leafhoppers and sawflies. Monitor the foliage for damage so that you can better deal with insects early on. See the Glossary of Pests & Diseases for advice.

John Franklin

Other names: none
Flower color: medium red
Flower size: 2½" (6.3 cm)
Scent: light, sweet
Height: 4–6' (1.2–1.8 m)
Spread: 4' (1.2 m)
Blooms: spring to fall, everblooming
Hardiness zones: 3–9

John Franklin has a slightly different flowering habit than other Explorer roses. It is an everblooming rose, meaning that it blooms continuously from summer to fall, rather than repeat blooming. It bears tight, hybrid tea–like buds that open to semi-double flowers. The small, fringed, medium red flowers are borne in abundant, large clusters of 30 or more. The leaves are serrated and dark green with touches of burgundy around their edges.

✿ Its compact, bushy form makes this rose ideal for hedging, borders, smaller gardens and any small areas that need a punch of color.
✿ This 1980 introduction was developed in Canada by Felicitas Svejada and bred from a cross between Lilli Marlene (a floribunda) and a hardy seedling that originated from Joanna Hill, Red Pinocchio and *Rosa spinosissima*.
✿ John Franklin is highly resistant to powdery mildew but is mildly susceptible to blackspot. It tolerates shade and requires little maintenance. Prune out deadwood if dieback has occurred.

This rose was named after a well-known British naval officer and northern explorer remembered for his expeditions and for the highly publicized 12-year search for him and his lost ships in the mid-1800s.

Lavender Lassie

L avender Lassie is a versatile rose that tolerates most soil and light conditions. It is valued as one of the few lavender-colored repeat-blooming shrubs. The blossoms open flat to jumbled centers, similar to the form of an old-fashioned rose. Though one of its parents was a hybrid musk, Lavender Lassie tends to behave more like a cluster-flowered rose. It grows into a strong, freely branched shrub bearing an abundance of semi-glossy foliage.

Other names: none
Flower color: medium pink with lavender
Flower size: 3" (7.6 cm)
Scent: strong, lilacs
Height: 5–7' (1.5–2.1 m)
Spread: 4–5' (1.2–1.5 m)
Blooms: summer to fall; repeat blooming
Hardiness zones: 4–9

✿ The large clusters are very weighty and dense enough to pull the branches down to the ground.
✿ Lavender Lassie is widely used because it is highly disease resistant and has an upright, vigorous nature. It tolerates poor soil and a little shade without the flower color suffering.
✿ In warmer regions the long canes can be trained to crawl up fences, walls or pillars. When left alone, Lavender Lassie is suitable as a specimen and planted in mixed beds or shrub borders.

Martin Frobisher

I ntroduced in 1968, Martin Frobisher was the first rose to be introduced in the Canadian Explorer series. It has the appearance of an old rose, bearing intensely fragrant, double, pale pink flowers that open from well-shaped buds. It is a vigorous, dense, compact, well-proportioned, pillar-shaped shrub. Dark red, smooth stems display wrinkly, grayish green leaves. This rose has some unique physical features—the older growth is covered in reddish brown bark, and the upper portions of the branches are spineless.

Other names: none

Flower color: pale pink

Flower size: 2¾" (7 cm)

Scent: strong, sweet

Height: 5–6' (1.5–1.8 m)

Spread: 4–5' (1.2–1.5 m)

Blooms: early summer to fall; repeat blooming

Hardiness zones: 2–9

❀ Unlike most Explorer roses, hips do not form on this rose once the flowers are finished.

❀ The foliage is prone to powdery mildew but resistant to blackspot.

❀ Deadheading may be necessary to keep the plant tidy, since the flowers cling, rather than fall cleanly from the plant, especially in wet weather.

Martin Frobisher was an Elizabethan seafaring explorer who discovered what is now known as Frobisher Bay on Baffin Island in 1576 as he was searching for the Northwest Passage.

Mary Rose

Mary Rose is one of the most bountiful and hardy of the Austin English roses. It bears medium pink flowers touched with lavender that darken with age. The bloom cycle is long, readily replacing one double, lightly fragrant flower after another. The blooms are borne at the tips of prickly arching stems covered in emerald green, matte foliage.

✿ Mary Rose is a great all-around shrub, ideal for group plantings, hedging and mixed borders. The classic, loose-petaled blooms mix well with a variety of other plants.

✿ This variety is not good for cutting, as the blooms are fragile and can shatter before they fully open.

✿ Mary Rose and its two sports are strong, disease resistant and tolerate most soils and exposures. The two sports are Winchester Cathedral, which bears pure white, fragrant flowers, and Redouté, a lighter pink rose.

✿ With its uneven growth habit, this rose may need to be reshaped with light pruning from one year to the next. Deadheading encourages further blooming.

Other names: none

Flower color:
medium pink

Flower size: 4–4½" (10–11 cm)

Scent: sweet honey and almonds

Height: 4–6' (1.2–1.8 m)

Spread: 4' (1.2 m)

Blooms: early summer to fall; repeat blooming

Hardiness zones: 5–9

This variety was introduced in 1983 and named after Henry VIII's flagship, recovered from the Solent River in England more than 400 years after it sank.

Morden Blush

It s pale pink, delicate blooms may lead you to believe that this rose is tender, but Morden Blush tolerates drought and extreme temperatures. It is heat and cold hardy, disease resistant and vigorous. It bears attractive buds that open flat into fully double sprays of rosette-shaped clusters. Each petal is infolded, forming into a muddled, button-shaped center. Cooler weather enhances the pale pink, while in hotter temperatures the color fades to ivory white. The matte green, semi-glossy foliage forms into a low-growing, bushy shrub and does not change color in fall. Once the flowers have finished for the season, hips follow.

Other names: none

Flower color: pale pink

Flower size: 1½–2" (4–5 cm)

Scent: light tea

Height: 24–36" (61–91 cm)

Spread: 24–36" (61–91 cm)

Blooms: spring to fall; everblooming

Hardiness zones: 2–9

✿ This Parkland series rose was introduced in 1988. Morden Blush is the longest blooming prairie-developed shrub rose to date. It was created by Collicutt & Marshall in Canada.

✿ Deadheading helps tidy the overall appearance of the plant during its blooming cycle. The flowers tend to look a little ragged as they come to an end.

✿ Morden Blush is mildly prone to powdery mildew and blackspot. Place it in a well-ventilated area, and water at the base of the plant in the morning.

The blooms are frequently used for corsages and bouquets, and landscape uses include mass plantings, borders and mixed beds.

Morden Fireglow

This rose is truly one of our favorites. One of the Parkland series, this hardy specimen bears flowers that aren't quite red yet not exactly orange—a color unlike that of any other hardy shrub rose. The formal flowers contrast beautifully with the dark, tough foliage. The upright form of Morden Fireglow is more like that of a hybrid tea than a modern shrub. The double blossoms form in loosely cupped sprays.

Other names: none
Flower color: deep, vivid red with orange
Flower size: 2–3" (5–7.6 cm)
Scent: light and mild
Height: 24–36" (61–91 cm)
Spread: 24–36" (61–91 cm)
Blooms: early summer to fall; repeat blooming
Hardiness zones: 2b–9

✿ This plant is considered self-cleaning because the petals fall cleanly from the plant once they've finished blooming.

✿ Morden Fireglow will stand out among a variety of sun-loving plants, making it ideal for mixed beds and borders. Cut the stems while the flowers are still buds to extend the longevity of the cut flowers in bouquets.

✿ Deadheading will increase the number of flowers. Stop deadheading in mid- to late summer to allow the plant to form hips and prepare for winter.

✿ The large globular hips remain on the plant well into the following spring.

✿ Pruning is required only to remove dead or diseased wood. Do not remove more than necessary but allow the flowers to emerge from both new and old wood.

Morden Ruby

The blooms of Morden Ruby are a unique blend of colors—not quite light pink and not quite dark pink, but a blend of dark and light flecks and tones. Some of the flowers change to solid colors or fade with age, but overall Morden Ruby flowers are notably different from other Parkland series rose blooms. This rose bears strong stems that support shiny, dark green leaves. Double clusters of flowers open from oval, reddish buds in late spring. The flowers are very long lasting, suitable for cutting and arrangements.

Other names: none

Flower color: mottled light and dark pink blend

Flower size: 3" (7.6 cm)

Scent: mild

Height: 3–4' (91–122 cm)

Spread: 4' (1.2 m)

Blooms: spring to fall; repeat blooming

Hardiness zones: 2–9

✿ Morden Ruby is vigorous and has moderate to good disease resistance but is somewhat prone to blackspot in areas with humid summers. Take all necessary precautions to prevent blackspot.

✿ Morden Ruby is naturally vigorous and somewhat lanky. If you want a bushier plant, prune hard in early spring, before the plant fully leafs out, by removing the longest rangy canes to the ground.

✿ It can be left as a beautiful specimen or mixed with a variety of blooming shrubs and perennials. Morden Ruby is suitable for just about any garden setting, including cottage gardens. It works well in more exposed areas where it could be forgotten occasionally.

Introduced in 1977, this rose is the sister of Adelaide Hoodless (p. 127).

Morden Snowbeauty

Morden Snowbeauty is the only white bloomer of the Parkland series and one of the most recent series introductions, released in 1998. It bears rather large, semi-double clusters of flowers exposing bright, yellow stamens. This low-spreading shrub is covered in shiny, dark green healthy foliage.

Other names: none
Flower color: white
Flower size: 3–4" (7.6–10 cm)
Scent: slight
Height: 3½' (1 m)
Spread: 3½' (1 m)
Blooms: early summer to fall; repeat blooming
Hardiness zones: 2b–8

✿ This extremely hardy specimen, created by Davidson & Collicutt of Canada, bears a large quantity of blooms in early summer, with inter-mittent flowers thereafter. A heavy second flush can be encouraged by a little deadheading and regular fertilizing.

✿ A mass of white roses is strikingly beautiful. This variety is also ideal for borders or left as a prolific specimen.

✿ The foliage is healthy, highly disease resistant and requires very little care or maintenance. This rose was selected by its breeders for its resistance to mildew and blackspot. What other testi-monials do you need?

Morden Sunrise

M orden Sunrise is an adorable semi-double rose. It was highly anticipated when it was introduced in 1999 and was very well received by the public. The first yellow variety in the Parkland series, it has a clean and fresh look, with blooms in tones of apricot and yellow along with attractive, shiny, dark green leaves.

Other names: none

Flower color: apricot yellow

Flower size: 3–3½" (7.6–9 cm)

Scent: mild

Height: 24–30" (61–76 cm)

Spread: 24–30" (61–76 cm)

Blooms: summer to fall; repeat blooming

Hardiness zone: 3–8

❀ With its compact size, erect stems and dense foliage, this rose is ideal for borders or mixed beds or as a specimen. Morden Sunrise is a colorful addition to just about any garden setting.

❀ Cooler temperatures cause the flower color to become more intense, while hotter weather results in paler, softer tones.

❀ Morden Sunrise has good early-season resistance to blackspot, powdery mildew and rust. The resistance to these problems dramatically decreases when humidity levels are higher or if it is planted in a damp location. Mildew problems can also be aggravated during times of drought, so make sure to water thoroughly when the need arises.

This rose bred for harsh winters performs beautifully in areas with mild winters as well.

Pat Austin

P at Austin is a modern English shrub rose introduced in 2002 by David Austin Roses Ltd. and
named in honor of Austin's wife, Pat, who is an
accomplished sculptor. It introduced a new vivid
color combination to the English rose series. Rich
copper shades are on the uppersides of the petals,
and pale amber yellow is on the undersides. Semi-
glossy, deep green foliage complements the large,
open, deeply cupped coppery flowers. The growth is
strong and slightly arching, similar to Abraham
Darby (p. 126). It would be difficult to miss the
exceptional contrasting tones as the strongly fragrant
flowers open and expand.

✿ Pat Austin is ideal as a medium-sized shrub.
   It can also be trained to become a short climber.
   It blends beautifully into mixed shrub borders,
   informal beds or containers.
✿ With its unique color, high level of disease resistance, graceful spreading form and strong and
   vigorous growth habit, this rose will likely
   become extremely popular.

Other names: none
Flower color: coppery
amber and yellow
Flower size: 2½–3½"
(6–9 cm)
Scent: fruity and sharp
Height: 3' (91 cm)
Spread: 4' (1.2 m)
Blooms: summer to fall;
repeat blooming
Hardiness zones: 5–9

*Pat Austin may be
difficult to find, as it
is such a recent intro-
duction, but it is well
worth looking for.*

Penelope

Penelope bears coppery peach buds that open to semi-double flowers touched with soft pinkish white. The large flower clusters are borne on plum-colored stems. The semi-glossy foliage has hints of bronze and darkens with age. It is considered one of Reverend J.H. Pemberton's best hybrid musk roses.

Other names: none
Flower color: blush pink
Flower size: 3" (7.6 cm)
Scent: sweet musk
Height: 4–5' (1.2–1.5 m)
Spread: 4–5' (1.2–1.5 m)
Blooms: summer to fall; repeat blooming
Hardiness zones: 3–11

✿ This rose is excellent for informal hedges or mixed borders. It can be left as a graceful, spreading shrub or pruned into a more compact specimen. Penelope is an elegant selection for Pacific Northwest gardens as it thrives throughout the west coast and the interior.

✿ Remove spent blooms to encourage repeat blooming.

✿ Introduced in 1924, Penelope has collected many honors and awards over the years, including the National Rose Society Gold Medal of 1925 and the 1993 Royal Horticultural Society Award of Garden Merit.

Roseraie de l'Haÿ

Roseraie de l'Haÿ reminds me of an elegant and compact version of Hansa, in form and bloom. The unforgettable scent carries on warm summer breezes. Considered one of the finest garden roses in its class, it is one of the most popular and widely grown rugosa roses. Its long, pointed buds open to large, double, crimson purple clusters. Unlike most rugosas, this variety rarely sets hips. The dense foliage is borne on heavily bristled, upright canes in a bushy form. Starting wrinkled and dark, the foliage changes to a deep red in fall.

Other names: none
Flower color:
rich crimson purple
Flower size: 4½" (11 cm)
Scent: cloves and cinnamon
Height: 7–9' (2.1–2.7 m)
Spread: 6' (1.8 m)
Blooms: summer to late fall; repeat blooming
Hardiness zones: 3–9

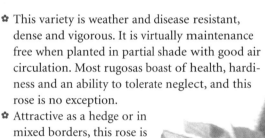

✿ This variety is weather and disease resistant, dense and vigorous. It is virtually maintenance free when planted in partial shade with good air circulation. Most rugosas boast of health, hardiness and an ability to tolerate neglect, and this rose is no exception.

✿ Attractive as a hedge or in mixed borders, this rose is often used in traditional garden settings, including cottage and English gardens.

✿ Spraying is not recommended when treating rugosas for disease. It is better to remove the diseased foliage or branches to allow for a flush of rejuvenated growth.

Sir Thomas Lipton

With its tolerance of cold, salt, shade, neglect and poor soil, Sir Thomas Lipton is versatile for the novice to advanced gardener. It is useful as a climber or small rambler. The spreading, vigorous and robust habit allows for training on arbors, trellises, pillars or doorways. The white double blooms atop leathery, dark foliage blend beautifully into cottage garden settings. It is also ideal for massing in borders, for large informal hedges or as a specimen when allowed enough room.

Other names: none
Flower color: white
Flower size: 2½–3" (6.3–7.6 cm)
Scent: strong
Height: 6–8' (1.8–2.4 m)
Spread: 5–7' (1.5–2.1 m)
Blooms: spring to fall; repeat blooming
Hardiness zones: 3–9

❀ Deadhead consistently through the growing season to extend the repeat blooming. Don't remove all flowers, as they will form into bright orange hips and add color to the fall landscape.

❀ A hard prune may be required to keep the fragrant flowers at eye level where they can be enjoyed.

❀ This rose was named after a yachtsman and entrepreneur from the late 1800s who challenged the America's Cup five years in a row without winning. He also developed different tea blends and invented the tea bag, thus signifigantly lowering the cost of what had been an expensive commodity.

The Fairy

The Fairy is trouble free and highly resistant to disease, requiring very little care. It is popular with novice to experienced gardeners. The moderately thorny canes are hidden by glossy foliage that forms into a compact and mounding form. It bears dainty, baby pink rosettes that develop into large clusters perched atop the leaves.

❀ A little pruning may be necessary to maintain The Fairy as a dwarf shrub. When left in its natural form, it grows into a delicate, spreading shrub. With light pruning, it can spread to almost 6' (1.8 m) wide on the coast but remains more compact in the interior.

❀ This rose is ideal for a variety of landscape purposes. It can be planted in containers or as a groundcover or left to trail over a low wall or embankment. It is easily trained as a weeping standard and integrates nicely into mixed beds and borders. It packs a punch when planted en masse or as low hedging. It also makes a beautiful cut flower.

❀ This rose blooms continually until fall frost.

The Fairy doesn't just tolerate neglect, it prefers it. It manages successfully in partial shade, and the shade slows the fading of the flower color.

Other names:
Fairy, Feerie

Flower color: soft pink

Flower size: 1–1½" (2.5–3.8 cm)

Scent: very little to light

Height: 24" (61 cm)

Spread: 24"–4' (61–122 cm)

Blooms: late summer to late fall; repeat blooming

Hardiness zones: 4–9

Thérèse Bugnet

Other names:
Theresa Bugnet

Flower color:
medium lilac pink

Flower size: 3–4"
(7.6–10 cm)

Scent: sweet cloves

Height: 5–6' (1.5–1.8 m)

Spread: 5–6' (1.5–1.8 m)

Blooms: summer to fall;
repeat blooming

Hardiness zones: 2–9

This variety was developed in Alberta by the late George Bugnet, who invested over 25 years creating this hybrid rugosa, which he then named after his daughter.

Thérèse Bugnet is a little hesitant to bloom when young but it's well worth the wait. Once established or at least two to three years of age, it will produce gray-green, rather smooth leaves on almost thornless canes. The stems are tipped with a profusion of ruffled, double, lilac pink blossoms that pale with age. After the flowers have all but finished, attractive fall color prevails, with cherry red canes, orange hips and bronzed foliage creating a distinctly beautiful shrub.

❀ This exceptional rugosa variety tolerates cold and heat, wind and late frosts. Thérèse Bugnet doesn't mind partial shade to full sun, alkaline, rocky, sandy or clay soils or neglect.

❀ One of the cold-hardiest roses in the world, this variety endures temperatures of –35° F (–37° C).

❀ Like other rugosas, Thérèse Bugnet resents being sprayed with fungicides. If mildew occurs, prune out and destroy infected growth.

❀ Deadheading regularly and pruning after the first flowering cycle in early summer will prolong the blooming cycle. Otherwise, the only pruning required would be to cut the magnificent flowers for arrangements.

❀ This rose has been known to bloom sparsely on the coast; some rose growers believe that it needs colder winter temperatures to bloom.

Vancouver Belle

Introduced in 1999, Vancouver Belle is a beautiful new introduction from one of the authors of this book—Brad Jalbert of Select Roses. It was chosen and named by the Vancouver Rose Society to celebrate its 50th anniversary. Flawless foliage is a stunning back-drop for the clear pink double blooms. It blooms early in summer and rapidly repeats blooming later in the season.

✿ It requires at least four hours a day of sunlight to produce the large clusters of flowers. Vancouver Belle tolerates just about any soil in practically any setting.

✿ This rose is ideal for containers, large tubs or barrels or in informal gardens.

✿ Very attractive in group plantings, Vancouver Belle also looks great when left as a specimen so that nothing else takes away from its faultless form.

Other names: none
Flower color: clear pink
Flower size: 4" (10 cm)
Scent: slight
Height: 24–36" (61–91 cm)
Spread: 24" (61 cm)
Blooms: summer to fall; repeat blooming
Hardiness zones: 4–9

This rose holds its form and color for a long time, making it ideal for cutting.

William Baffin

Other names: none
Flower color: deep pink
Flower size: 2½–3"
(6.3–7.6 cm)
Scent: little to none
Height: 8–10' (2.4–3 m)
Spread: 5–6' (1.5–1.8 m)
Blooms: summer to fall;
repeat blooming
Hardiness zones: 2–9

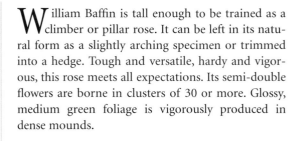

William Baffin is tall enough to be trained as a climber or pillar rose. It can be left in its natural form as a slightly arching specimen or trimmed into a hedge. Tough and versatile, hardy and vigorous, this rose meets all expectations. Its semi-double flowers are borne in clusters of 30 or more. Glossy, medium green foliage is vigorously produced in dense mounds.

❀ William Baffin is a truly impressive specimen. It is hardy enough to remain on a trellis, arbor or pergola in the coldest of winters, without pruning or any special winter protection. It can grow quite tall in milder climates.

❀ Overall William Baffin is highly disease resistant and requires very little to no maintenance.

❀ This rose was named after the famous explorer who in 1616 discovered Lancaster Sound when he was trying to find the Northwest Passage. Robert Bylot accompanied Baffin on this voyage, and they sailed farther north than any other explorer would for the next 236 years.

It might be easier to enjoy the intensely fragrant flowers if the plant is pruned to a lower height.

Winnipeg Parks

This rose has been difficult to come by in recent years, because it is so popular that rose growers couldn't grow plants fast enough to meet consumer demand. The flower color is similar to that of Alexander Mackenzie (p. 129), though Winnipeg Parks has a slightly different form. It bears pointed buds that open into velvety, cupped, double clusters of reddish pink, lightly scented blossoms. The striking color of the flowers contrasts well with the matte, medium green foliage. It quickly forms into a tight, dense, compact form and has the most attractive foliage of the Parkland series.

Other names: none
Flower color:
deep, vivid, pinky red
Flower size: 3½" (9 cm)
Scent: slight
Height: 12–36"
(30–91 cm)
Spread: 12–24"
(30–61 cm)
Blooms: summer to fall; repeat blooming
Hardiness zones: 2–9

✿ In cooler weather the green leaves can be tinted with red.

✿ This variety is suitable for bedding, borders or as a specimen. Winnipeg Parks grows very close to the ground, so it is ideal for the edges of mixed flower beds and containers. As with most of the Canadian-bred roses, Winnipeg Parks can get much larger in mild areas of the Pacific Northwest unless kept in check by pruning each season.

✿ The disease resistance is moderate to good, and the foliage shouldn't require any special attention to prevent disease.

✿ This 1990 introduction was named after the City of Winnipeg's Parks and Recreation department in honor of its 1993 centennial.

Unfortunately the flowers don't last terribly long, so deadhead to encourage further blooming. The flowers can also be cut in the early stages for arrangements, crafts or recipes.

GROUNDCOVER

These roses are not groundcovers in the true sense of the word but are a good choice for large areas that need color. Generally groundcover roses remain small and have a procumbent or spreading habit. The best groundcover roses send down roots where the canes touch the ground. Some hardy, low-growing hybrids have been developed recently that work very well for this purpose. Smaller, hardy shrub roses can also be mass planted to fill a large area with color.

Dwarf Pavement

Other names: Dwf.
Pavement, Rosazwerg
Flower color:
medium pink
Flower size: 3" (7.6 cm)
Scent: intense
Height: 24"–5'
(61 cm–1.5 m)
Spread: 18–24"
(46–61 cm)
Blooms: summer to fall;
repeat blooming
Hardiness zones: 3–9

*By sending out side
shoots, this rose can
sometimes reach
widths of 6' (1.8 m)*

P avement roses were originally created in Germany to use alongside busy roadways and are now being used in a similar way in North America. These roses can be used as groundcovers, foundation plantings, informal low hedges or in mixed beds and borders. Dwarf Pavement grows in a compact form low to the ground. It bears semi-double, medium pink flowers that bloom repeatedly through summer. Deep, scarlet hips follow the flowers in fall and remain on the plant well into winter.

❀ The wrinkly textured, medium green foliage has a strong resistance to blackspot and mildew.

❀ Pruning and spraying are simply not required, as this rose can plainly take care of itself. Pavement roses are usually on their own rootstock, which only improves their hardiness.

❀ Dwarf Pavement is hardy and versatile and tolerates heat and salt. It thrives on the coast. Deadhead regularly throughout the season, but stop deadheading five to six weeks before a hard fall frost to allow the shrub to set hips and prepare for winter.

Foxy Pavement

Foxy Pavement has award-winning fragrance, colorful flowers and disease-resistant foliage. This hybrid rugosa has large, semi-double flowers among deeply textured, medium green foliage. Dark hips follow the flowers and remain on the plant until the following spring.

✿ This rose has a compact, mounded form, and the spreading, low branches can extend farther than normal in very rich soil. Its tolerance of pruning makes it suitable for low hedging and borders. It has a tidy habit and is more compact than other rugosas. It also has an excellent repeat blooming cycle.

✿ Foxy Pavement tolerates tough conditions and doesn't resent extreme temperatures or salt.

✿ Deadheading isn't required for further blooming, and the hips will begin to form while the flowers are still being produced, resulting in an interesting visual contrast.

Other names: Buffalo Gal, Foxi Pavement

Flower color: dark pink

Flower size: 3" (7.6 cm)

Scent: spicy and very strong

Height: 30–36" (76–91 cm)

Spread: 30" (76 cm)

Blooms: summer to fall; repeat blooming

Hardiness zones: 3–9

Foxy Pavement looks similar to Frau Dagmar Hastrup (p.138) but has a smaller form and deeply pink flowers.

Pierette Pavement

Other names:
Yankee Lady
Flower color: dark pink
Flower size: 4" (10 cm)
Scent: exceptionally
strong, cloves
Height: 3–4' (91–122 cm)
Spread: 24–36"
(61–91 cm)
Blooms: summer to fall;
repeat blooming
Hardiness zones: 2–9

*This rose was
developed by Uhl
of Germany in 1997.
Its German name
includes the German
word for 'bedding,'
reflecting its most com-
mon use in Germany
as a bedding plant.*

Its vivid blooms and striking fall color make Pierette Pavement slightly different than other pavement roses, but it does share some of the characteristics of pavement roses, including the long bloom period. Pierette Pavement begins to bloom in early summer and continues well into fall. It bears masses of semi-double flowers and textured, medium green foliage. The blooms are large and have an adorable button eye.

✿ With its low-growing, spreading habit, this pavement rose is ideal as a groundcover, in borders or as low hedging.

✿ With its ability to tolerate salt and extreme temperatures, this rose thrives in a coastal environment.

✿ Large quantities of hips are produced in summer and well into winter, remaining on the shrub until spring. The hips can attract various forms of wildlife during winter.

Purple Pavement

P urple Pavement bears semi-double, showy clusters of fragrant flowers held in small trusses. The yellow stamens are especially prominent among the deep purple-red flowers and medium green, textured foliage. Dark red hips are produced during and after the flowering cycles, and the foliage slowly evolves into a blast of fall color.

❁ Purple Pavement is frequently used in massed bushy borders, as hedging or just left on its own as a specimen. It thrives in full sun to partial shade. It will continue to grow in less sunlight, though it won't be as vigorous. This rose doesn't really require any maintenance, making it an ideal variety to display and enjoy.

❁ Purple Pavement was developed by Baum in Germany. It proved how versatile, hardy, disease resistant and low maintenance these colorful hybrid rugosas are.

Other names: Rotesmeer, Rotsmere, Exception

Flower color: purple red

Flower size: 3" (7.6 cm)

Scent: strong

Height: 3–4' (91–122 cm)

Spread: 30"–4' (76–122 cm)

Blooms: summer to fall; repeat blooming

Hardiness zones: 3–9

This rose tolerates extreme temperatures and salt so is useful in a coastal environment.

Scarlet Pavement

Other names: Rote Apart
Flower color: reddish pink
Flower size: 2–3"
(5–7.6 cm)
Scent: strong
Height: 30"–3½'
(76–107 cm)
Spread: 30"–3½'
(76–107 cm)
Blooms: summer to fall;
repeat blooming
Hardiness zones: 2–9

When it was introduced in 1991, Scarlet Pavement expanded the colors of pavement roses. The shapely pink buds open to semi-double clusters of red flowers intermittently through summer. Healthy, medium green, glossy, textured foliage is produced on spreading, outstretched stems. The golden stamens stand out against the scarlet petals, which are replaced in fall by dark red hips.

✿ Similar to the other varieties in the series, Scarlet Pavement tolerates extreme temperatures and salt, making it ideal for coastal plantings.

✿ This variety is useful for massed plantings, borders or hedges or as a specimen. Pruning, deadheading and spraying are all unnecessary, allowing you to enjoy the rose rather than hover over it.

Developed by Uhl in Germany, Scarlet Pavement is a cross from Frau Dagmar Hastrup (p. 138) and Moje Hammarberg.

Snow Pavement

This 1986 introduction has some unusual characteristics compared to others in the series. The flower color, white tinged with tones of mauve and pink, is original. The large-petaled, double flowers open from long, pale pink buds. The bright green, textured foliage is very tough, healthy and disease resistant and moderately paler than that of other pavement roses.

❈ Red hips are produced towards the latter part of summer into fall and remain on the plant until the following spring.

❈ This rose's low-growing, spreading, bushy habit makes it ideal for low hedging, in a border or as a specimen. In very rich soil, pruning may be needed to keep the plant compact and under control. Deadheading is unnecessary.

❈ This variety tolerates salt, extreme temperatures and poor soil. It is a little more prone to disease than other pavement roses.

Other names:
Schneekoppe
Flower color:
white, tinged mauve pink
Flower size: 3" (7.6 cm)
Scent: powerful
Height: 3–4'
(91–122 cm)
Spread: 36" (91 cm)
Blooms: summer to fall;
repeat blooming
Hardiness zones: 3–9

The flowers have been known to appear glowing white at dusk, making this rose a very pretty addition to just about any garden setting.

CLIMBERS & RAMBLERS

C limbing roses do not in fact climb. The canes must be trained and tied into place on some form of support. Climbers generally have long, stiff, arching canes ranging in length from 8 to 15' (2.4 to 4.6 m). The canes are productive for more than two seasons and often become thick and woody.

Climbing roses come from various sources, and the hardiness of a variety depends on its parentage. For just about any climate or region, there is a climber, including climbing hybrid teas and climbing Explorer series roses. Pruning practices can greatly influence the form of your climbing rose. Vigorous shrubs can be pruned to encourage climbing, and climbers can be pruned to resemble shrubs.

Hybrid teas, floribundas, grandifloras and other bush or shrub roses sometimes mutate to produce long, vigorous canes, referred to as sports. Climbing sports produce the same flower types and blooming habits of the roses they sported from. Some seedlings are grown and propagated as a source of climbers. The more recent introductions are less rampant than the older types and are repeat blooming. The canes terminate in an inflorescence, later flowering from laterals produced on the main canes.

Ramblers have longer flexible canes that can reach lengths of 20' (6 m) or more. Rambler canes behave like raspberry canes in that new canes grow without flowering for their first season, and flowers are produced along the canes in the second season. When the flowering cycle is complete, the canes should be pruned out. Ramblers need to be tied to a support when trained to grow in an upright direction. They can also be left to 'ramble' along the ground or to trail down an embankment or stone wall.

Early climbers and ramblers arose from crossing hybrid teas and other classes mainly with *Rosa wichuraiana* and *Rosa multiflora*. They bloomed once a year and were often rampant

growers. *Rosa wichuraiana* is in the ancestry of many modern climbers, and there are still many non-repeat Wichuraiana climbers available in commerce.

Altissimo

American Pillar

Adélaïde d'Orléans

Other names:
Léopoldine d'Orléans

Flower color:
pale pinkish white

Flower size: 1–2"
(2.5–5 cm)

Scent: strong and
sweet primrose

Height: 15' (4.6 m)

Spread: 10' (3 m)

Blooms: mid-summer;
repeat blooming

Hardiness zones: 5–11

*This rose received the
Royal Horticultural
Society Award of
Garden Merit in 1993.*

Antoine Jacques, who created this rose in 1826, was the head gardener to the Duc d'Orléans at Château de Neuilly, and later to the duke's son, who became King Louis-Phillipe. Jacques used *Rosa sempervirens* to create the small but select group of roses we now call Sempervirens Hybrids. Once almost lost to cultivation, Adélaïde d'Orléans is one of these Sempervirens ramblers. It grows in all directions on thin, red-prickled rambling canes. The neat foliage is tinged with purple, and the rosy pink buds open to pale white flowers with showy yellow stamens.

✿ Adélaïde d'Orléans tolerates poorer soils and shade. It is generally disease resistant but a little susceptible to mildew, especially during drought. Considered almost evergreen in locations with warmer winters, it tends to be more vulnerable where an exceptional freeze is possible.

✿ Pergolas, doorways, arches, fences or trellises are perfect locations for this variety, which provides a fine display from top to bottom. In full bloom, this is one of the most beautiful ramblers, as the flowers cover every inch of the plant. It suffers little dieback even after experiencing cold.

✿ The flowers emerge in a heavy flush in mid-summer with a sporadic repeat blooming in fall.

Albéric Barbier

Albéric Barbier was the first in a long line of prominent ramblers developed and released by Barbier et Compagnie of Orléans. It is very disease resistant and requires virtually no pruning or care. This Wichuraiana rambler bears creamy yellow buds that open to off white, large flowers in small clusters. The flowers are supported by slender, flexible stems and nearly evergreen shiny, dark green foliage. Albéric Barbier is extremely vigorous and tolerates shade and poor soil.

❀ This rose is suitable for twining up trees and pergolas or as a groundcover or weeping standard. It will easily climb up to 20' (6.1 m) when trained. It is a poor choice for climbing walls because the reduced air circulation around the plant encourages mildew.

❀ Albéric Barbier was honored 93 years after its original introduction with the Royal Horticultural Society Award of Garden Merit in 1993.

Other names: none

Flower color:
creamy light yellow

Flower size: 3–3½" (7.6–9 cm)

Scent: fruity apple, sweet

Height: 15–20' (4.6–6.1 m)

Spread: 12–15' (3.6–4.6 m)

Blooms: early to mid-summer; no repeat blooming

Hardiness zones: 4–10

Enjoy the profuse creamy flowers while they last— the repeat blooming cycle is unreliable.

Albertine

Other names: none
Flower color:
salmon pink
Flower size: 3" (7.6 cm)
Scent: richly fragrant
Height: 15–20'
(4.5–6.1 m)
Spread: 15' (4.5 m)
Blooms: mid-summer;
no repeat blooming
Hardiness zones: 5–9

Albertine is an aggressive rambler suitable for covering a fence, pergola or the side of a house. It is also effective as an unsupported specimen shrub. Its reddish buds open to delicate, salmon pink blooms made up of an average of 25 petals each. The clusters of richly scented flowers are borne on the tips of plum-colored, arching branches. Glossy, striking purplish green foliage fills out to create a dense form.

✿ It flowers for approximately three to four weeks in mid-summer.
✿ The stems may require repeated securing as the plant reaches its mature height and spread.
✿ Generally disease resistant, Albertine is a little prone to mildew in drier climates and seasons.

Albertine was developed in 1921 by René Barbier of Barbier & Cie in Orléans, France. In 1993 it was awarded the Royal Horticultural Society Award of Merit.

Altissimo

*A*ltissimo is Italian for 'in the highest.' It is an apt name for this climbing floribunda, which grows high, is of high quality and is highly disease resistant. Large, matte, leathery, dark, serrated foliage complements the nearly flat, deeply colored flowers. The large blooms are borne on new and old growth. Altissimo is considered one of the best red climbers and one of the easiest climbers to grow. The single flowers almost obscure the plant throughout the season.

Other names:
Altus, Sublimely Single
Flower color:
crisp, blood red
Flower size: 5 " (13 cm)
Scent: slight
Height: 10–14' (3–4.3 m)
Spread: 8' (2.4 m)
Blooms: early summer; repeat blooming
Hardiness zones: 4–9

✿ Remove the spent blooms to encourage long-term, prolific blooming. The nearly rounded, blood red petals sometimes fall off soon after the large, single flowers have opened.

✿ When cut, the blooms keep well with unfading color and are useful in a variety of arrangements.

✿ In a warm location, it has been known to grow large enough to cover the side of a one-story building. In a cooler location, Altissimo doesn't grow as large.

✿ This rose can be grown successfully as a large shrub if pruned hard and given room to fill out. If trained as a climber, it will require support on a pillar, pergola, veranda post or trellis. The stiff and sturdy stems create an upright, bushy and spreading form suitable for just about any garden setting.

George Delbard of Delbard-Chabert developed this stately climber in 1966 in France. Altissimo is a seedling of Tenor, a red climber also created by Delbard.

American Pillar

Other names: none

Flower color: bright carmine pink; white centers

Flower size: 2–3" (5–7.6 cm)

Scent: light to none

Height: 15–20' (4.5–6.1 m)

Spread: 10–12' (3–3.6 m)

Blooms: mid-spring to mid-summer; no repeat blooming

Hardiness zones: 4–9

Despite its name, American Pillar is considered too aggressive to be a pillar rose and is better suited to climb up the side of a house, pergola, wire fence or lattice or to twine through an old, sturdy tree. It bears large clusters of small, deep pink flowers with prominent yellow stamens. Elongated, thick, arching stems support long-lasting blooms that fade from deep to light pink with age. The blooms have a tendency to be mottled by rain. Bright red oval hips and bronze fall foliage follow the summer flowers.

✿ Though this rose begins to bloom a little later than most ramblers, the flowers last a long time. The flowers are perfect for cutting and simple arrangements.

✿ This rose has more impact if it is allowed to grow to its mature height rather than being pruned into a smaller shrub. Once established, it requires little attention.

✿ Relatively disease free, American Pillar is somewhat prone to powdery mildew in locations with poor air circulation.

This rose is ideal for a coastal setting. It tolerates shade and poor soils but resents hot, dry weather.

Bobbie James

B obbie James is best grown where it can reach its full mature height and spread. As a giant rambler requiring substantial support, Bobbie James will eventually cover a three-car garage or an outbuilding. It is also very attractive when allowed to twine through an old sturdy tree.

Other names: none
Flower color: creamy white
Flower size: 2" (5 cm)
Scent: sweet
Height: 28–30' (8.5–9 m)
Spread: 20' (6.1 m)
Blooms: mid-summer; no repeat blooming
Hardiness zones: 5–9

❀ Seeing this rose's once-yearly bloom is memorable. It blooms profusely for an average of four to six weeks in mid-summer, bearing thousands of semi-double, cupped blooms in copious, drooping clusters made up of 50 blooms or more. The creamy white petals surround showy golden stamens. Long, thick, prickly stems carry an abundance of glossy, deep green leaves with coppery edges.
❀ The sweet fragrance of the blooms permeates the garden.
❀ Introduced in 1961 and popular ever since, this rose was named for a renowned Yorkshire horticulturist, regarded as one of the grand old men of gardening.

Brad has a seven-year-old plant that is approximately 40' (12 m) tall, growing up the trunk of an old giant cedar. It has never been sprayed for disease, fertilized or pruned. It blooms like crazy and is healthy as could be.

Chevy Chase

Chevy Chase bears small, double, crimson red flowers that form into tight, full clusters. The flowers contrast beautifully with the light gray-green, wrinkled foliage on stiff canes clothed with hooked prickles. This unusual rambler was bred from a *Rosa soulineana* rather than a *Rosa wichuraiana* lineage.

Other names: none
Flower color:
deep crimson red
Flower size: 2–2½"
(5–6.3 cm)
Scent: moderate to strong
Height: 15' (4.5 m)
Spread: 8' (2.4 m)
Blooms: mid-summer;
no repeat blooming
Hardiness zones: 5–9

❀ This vigorous plant reaches its mature height in one season once fully established. It may require a little maintenance, including pruning and deadheading, for the best effect. Wait until the flowering cycle is complete before pruning. The long-lasting, fragrant blooms are ideal for cutting and arranging.
❀ Chevy Chase can be trained on a fence to create privacy, but the canes are quite stiff and difficult to work with.
❀ This rose is disease resistant but a little prone to rust.
❀ Introduced in 1939, Chevy Chase won the Dr. W. Van Fleet Medal in 1941. It was named after the city in Maryland where it was raised by N.J. Hansen.

Good red rambling roses are hard to find, and this one has experienced increased popularity. Chevy Chase is in high demand throughout the coast as it is one of the best overall ramblers for a coastal environment.

City of York

City of York, developed during World War II and named after a city in Pennsylvania, well deserves its accolades, including the ARS National Gold Medal Certificate it received in 1950. It bears large clusters of creamy white, semi-double, saucer-shaped flowers surrounding bright yellow stamens. The rich flowers emerge from the tips of long, arching, pliable canes clothed in glossy, deep green foliage. Large hips follow the flowers, so this rose is attractive well into winter.

Other names:
Direcktör Benschop

Flower color:
creamy white

Flower size: 3–3½" (7.6–9 cm)

Scent: strong and citrus

Height: 20' (6.1 m)

Spread: 12' (3.7 m)

Blooms: mid-season; no repeat blooming

Hardiness zones: 5–9

❀ City of York tolerates full sun, but in semi-shade it thrives and the flowers remain on the plant with very little discoloration.

❀ Because the growth habit of this rose is more like that of a rambler than a climber, it is best for growing up pergolas, trellises and pillars instead of walls or flat surfaces.

❀ It is relatively disease and maintenance free, easy to grow, extremely vigorous and produces a large crop of hips. Provide City of York and most other climbing roses with adequate air circulation to discourage potential disease.

Compassion

Compassion was introduced in 1973 by Harkness in England. This solid performer has set the standard for climbing roses, as it has great color and is fragrant, easy to maintain and disease resistant. Its well-shaped buds open to double, rounded clusters of tightly packed petals. The flowers are very durable and exhibit good color, which can vary according to weather conditions.

Other names:
Belle de Londres
Flower color:
soft salmon, apricot
Flower size: 4½–5"
(11–13 cm)
Scent: rich, strong and sweet
Height: 10–15' (3–4.6 m)
Spread: 5–8' (1.5–2.4 m)
Blooms: summer to fall; repeat blooming
Hardiness zones: 4–9

❀ Especially useful for climbing up walls, pillars or fences, this rose is also good for mixed beds and borders. Because it blooms well on new wood, it can be pruned and trained as a large shrub. If you want to use it as a smaller specimen, pruning may be necessary to control its size. Follow the recommended practice for pruning a climber. Pruning after the blooming period has finished will not increase the level of flower production in the subsequent flush of blooms.

❀ It is generally disease resistant, but mildew can be a problem where air circulation is poor.

❀ The long, sturdy stems yield large, red thorns that are somewhat showy and make a nice contrast to the hips throughout winter.

❀ Highfield is a pale yellow sport of Compassion.

The blooms, borne singly or in clusters of three flowers per stem, are reminiscent of hybrid tea blossoms.

Constance Spry

Constance Spry was created in 1961 and named after the famous floral arranger, author and collector of old garden roses from the 1950s to 1960s. It was the first English rose that David Austin created. It bears extremely large, cupped, fully double, soft pink flowers. The showy blooms blend well with the plentiful, semi-glossy, coarse, grayish green leaves. This rose bears one large profusion of blossoms, with no repeat bloom, so you must appreciate the strongly fragrant flowers while they are in bloom.

Other names:
Constanze Spry
Flower color: soft pink
Flower size: 5" (13 cm)
Scent: strong myrrh
Height: 12–15'
(3.5–4.5 m)
Spread: 5–6' (1.5–1.8 m)
Blooms: mid-summer;
no repeat blooming
Hardiness zones: 4b–9

✿ This rose blooms with or without care or attention. It prefers moderately fertile soil and cooler climates but tolerates light shade, long hot summers and neglect. It is highly disease resistant.

✿ Once the flowers are finished, a light pruning may be needed to keep the plant from growing too large.

✿ Ideal for climbing walls, heavy lattices or pergolas, this rose can also be used at the back of a mixed border or as a large shrub or specimen. Support of some kind is necessary to reinforce the vigorous, sprawling, arching stems.

I have grown this rose in partial shade and poor soil for many years and have never fertilized or watered it in summer.
— Brad Jalbert

Dortmund

Other names: none
Flower color:
red with a white eye
Flower size: 3–4"
(7.6–10 cm)
Scent: light apple
Height: 14–24'
(4.3–7.3 m)
Spread: 8–10' (2.4–3 m)
Blooms: spring to fall;
repeat blooming
Hardiness zones: 5–9

*This rose was intro-
duced in 1955 by
Kordes from Germany
and named after the
city of Dortmund.*

F ew roses are rated as highly and respected as
much as Dortmund, which has many excellent
qualities. It grows tall and upright but dense in form.
It bears large, single, deep red flowers with a glowing
central white eye and bright yellow stamens. The single flowers have an average of five to seven petals.
Dark glossy foliage complements the flower color.
The foliage alone makes Dortmund worth having in
the garden.

✿ Dortmund requires reasonably good growing
conditions to thrive. It is a little slow to bloom in
spring, but once it begins to take off, the results
are worth the wait.

✿ This rose can grow large enough to cover one
side of a small building. To create a medium
shrub useful for hedging or as a specimen, prune
to control the size. As a climber it can be trained
up a pillar, veranda post, wall or trellis. It can also
be grafted as a weeping standard.

✿ Deadhead heavily and frequently to encourage
blooming. Discontinue deadheading at least five
weeks before first frost to allow the plant to form
a large crop of bright red hips in fall.

✿ Dortmund tolerates light, dappled shade and
poorer soils and is highly
disease resistant.

✿ Dortmund has
received many awards
including the Portland
Gold Medal in 1971
and the Anerkannte
Deutsche Rose Award
in 1954.

Dublin Bay

Dublin Bay is one of the best red-bloomed climbers available. It blooms longer and more frequently than just about any other climber. The first flush of blooms can last six weeks or more. On the west coast it bears stunning blossoms throughout the season. It has a reliable growth habit and weatherproof flowers and is low maintenance and highly disease resistant. Large oval buds emerge in spring on new and old wood and open to well-shaped, double blooms. The moderately thorny stems support dark green, shiny foliage.

Other names: Grandhotel
Flower color: bright red
Flower size: 4½" (11 cm)
Scent: moderate to strong
Height: 8–14' (2.4–4.3 m)
Spread: 5–7' (1.5–2.1 m)
Blooms: summer to fall; repeat blooming
Hardiness zones: 4–11

✿ Dublin Bay fans out well on low fences and trellises. It is attractive climbing up tripods, pillars, pergolas or arches. It can also be pruned into an informal hedge.
✿ This rose prefers full sun and moist, well-drained soil. It holds up well in cold or heat but should not be planted in windy locations.
✿ Dublin Bay was bred by Sam McGredy IV of New Zealand. Its color and structure come from Altissimo, and its free-flowering nature from its other parent, Bantry Bay. It was introduced in 1975 and won the Royal Horticultural Society Award of Garden Merit in 1993.

The rich, long-lasting flowers hold their color well even when cut for crafts or arrangements.

François Juranville

François Juranville is one of the most common and most beautiful Wichuraiana Hybrids. It bears apple-scented, salmon pink and pale yellow quilled flowers. Shiny, dark green leaves with bronzed edges are borne on upright, vigorous canes.

Other names: none
Flower color: yellow with salmon pink
Flower size: 3" (7.6 cm)
Scent: fruity apple
Height: 25' (7.6 m)
Spread: 15' (4.5 m)
Blooms: mid-summer; no repeat blooming
Hardiness zones: 4–9

✿ Minimal care is required. Prune just after the flowering cycle is complete, removing the oldest, woodiest growth right down to the ground. Failing to do this will result in a mass of entangled deadwood in the center, which will make the plant less attractive and more vulnerable to mildew. Powdery mildew can occur occasionally after flowering. It doesn't seem to harm the plant, however, and rarely affects the flowering.
✿ This rose variety is most useful scaling up a tree, pergola or trellis but, unsupported, has been widely used as a groundcover as well. It is best in partial shade where the flower color appears more intense.

Introduced in 1906, François Juranville received the Royal Horticultural Society Award of Garden Merit in 1993.

Ghislaine de Feligonde

I n excellent conditions Ghislaine de Feligonde will continually produce bright yellow buds that open into light yellow blossoms. The flowers, borne in massive clusters, may change from yellow to pink, orange, salmon or red. The clusters average 10–20 flowers each, and each flower consists of 20–40 petals and exposes large, prominent stamens. Attractive red hips follow the flowers in late summer to fall. Medium green, glossy leaves cover the nearly thorn-less canes. The foliage provides spectacular orangy brown shades in fall.

Other names: none

Flower color: apricot tinged with pink

Flower size: 1½–2" (3.8–5 cm)

Scent: moderately sweet

Height: 15–20' (4.5–6.1 m)

Spread: 10–15' (3–4.5 m)

Blooms: spring to summer; repeat blooming

Hardiness zones: 5–9

❀ This extraordinary but scarcely known rose is extremely vigorous and grows to massive heights if supported. It is suitable for climbing on arbors, trellises and archways and is exceptional as a cut flower. It is spectacular when allowed to cascade down walls and embankments. It can be trained as a large shrub reaching up to 7' (2.1 m) tall and 8' (2.4 m) wide without support.

❀ This variety tolerates shade and poor soil conditions and doesn't mind a little pruning.

Ghislaine de Feligonde is growing in popularity but its unusual name seems to relegate it to being a more 'obscure' rose.

Handel

Handel is one of the most delicate climbing roses available. It is stunning in full bloom, displaying a profusion of semi-double, white and creamy-centered blossoms edged in deep pink. The slender buds open to loosely double, wavy blooms in mid-summer and bloom less frequently as fall approaches. The glossy, dark foliage is only mildly affected by blackspot, and the flowers can withstand a rainfall without any damage. It begins to develop slowly but gradually increases in vigor and performance as it ages.

Other names:
Haendel, Händel, Macha

Flower color:
white; pink edges

Flower size: 3½–4" (9–10 cm)

Scent: little to none

Height: 12–15' (3–3.6 m)

Spread: 4–8' (1.2–2.4 m)

Bloom period: summer to fall; repeat blooming

Hardiness zones: 5–9

Handel has received many awards including the Portland Gold Medal in 1975.

❀ This rose is a strong grower, and the upright, stiff stems are best growing on a fence, wall, arbor or pergola. Handel can be trained as a shrub with moderate pruning. The pruning will not affect the blooming cycles, as this rose bears flowers on new and old wood.

❀ The mid-season blooms sometimes look ragged, but a little deadheading will take care of that and will also encourage further flowering in larger quantities.

❀ The young flowers are neatly formed and high centered, reminiscent of hybrid tea blooms, and then open cupped in wide clusters. These blooms look best when grown in a cooler location or during cooler periods.

Laura Ford

Laura Ford is a simple yet elegant yellow rose. It is resistant to disease, easy to maintain and grow, produces weatherproof blooms and is a good example of a modern miniature climber. What more could you ask for? The soft yellow blooms touched with pale pink form into semi-double, dense clusters that vary in shades with age. Shiny, small, medium green leaves complement the flowers on a tall, upright, well-branched framework.

❁ This rose is suitable as a climber on low walls, pillars, fences or trellises. It is ideal as a specimen for average garden settings.

❁ No pruning is required, and large hips set well into fall, which is unusual for a miniature rose. Deadheading will encourage a lengthy flush of blooms.

❁ This variety was named after a well-known English artist. It received the Royal National Rose Society Certificate of Merit in 1988 and the Royal Horticultural Society Award of Garden Merit in 1993.

❁ Laura Ford doesn't require any special conditions or care. It is a relatively hardy miniature climber, ideal for any gardener or rose aficionado.

Other names: Normandie, King Tut

Flower color: soft yellow; pale pink edges

Flower size: 2" (5 cm)

Scent: moderate, sweet and fruity

Height: 7' (2.1 m)

Spread: 4' (1.2 m)

Blooms: spring to fall; repeat blooming

Hardiness zones: 5–9

This is one of my favorite roses, and not only because we have the same first name. I especially love the burgundy buds and stems that contrast so beautifully with the lemony blossoms that in turn showcase amber stamens.
— Laura Peters

Lichtkönigen Lucia

Other names: Lucia, Reine Lucia, Light Queen Lucia, Lichtkönigin Lucia

Flower color: canary yellow

Flower size: 3–4" (7.6–10 cm)

Scent: slight yet sweet

Height: 8–10' (2.4–3 m)

Spread: 3–4' (91–122 cm)

Blooms: summer to fall; repeat blooming

Hardiness zone: 4–9

L ichtkönigen Lucia, introduced in 1966, is not used as much as it should be considering its many positive and unique characteristics. From early summer to fall it continually bears flushes of large, shallow, saucer-shaped, double-clustered blossoms. The bright yellow flowers showcase red stamens and do not fade. Strong thornless stems are clothed in large, wrinkled, glossy, dark leaves.

❀ This versatile rose has a tall, upright and free-branching growth habit, making it suitable for mixed borders. It can also be trained as a specimen or as a short climber in milder climates. Lichtkönigen Lucia is considered one of the most winter-hardy yellow climbers available.

❀ The foliage is healthy and resistant to just about anything that comes its way. It tolerates poorer soil and a little neglect.

❀ This rose received the Anerkannte Deutsche Rose Award in 1968.

Lichtkönigen Lucia is German for 'Lucia, Queen of Light,' a reference to its vibrant yellow shades. It is colorful enough to brighten any spot requiring some intensity.

Madame Alfred Carriere

Madame Alfred Carriere is considered one of the best noisettes ever developed. It was introduced in 1879, somewhat later than most other noisettes. It can still be found climbing the high wall of a cottage in Sissinghurst Castle Garden in Kent in southern England. It bears clusters of long-lasting, flattish double flowers. The flowers open from pink pearl buds that are suitable for cutting. Each petal has a touch of yellow at the base, but only towards the center of the blossom. Large, semi-glossy leaves with serrated edges are vigorously produced on smooth, arching stems, resulting in upright, strong growth.

Other names: none

Flower color: creamy white

Flower size: 2½–3" (6.4–7.6 cm)

Scent: sweet, fresh and tea-like

Height: 15–18' (4.6–5.5 m)

Spread: 10–12' (3–3.7 m)

Blooms: summer to fall; repeat blooming

Hardiness zones: 4–9

❀ Mildew can be a problem, but this rose is generally disease resistant and maintenance free.

❀ This reliable rose is excellent for climbing walls, old trees, trellises or pergolas. The flexible, arching canes allow for easy training, and this rose can be trained as a hedge.

❀ Madame Alfred Carriere tolerates some shade or a north wall, although the flowering will not be as profuse as it would be in a bright and sunny location. It is moderately winter hardy and better left unpruned.

❀ This rose was bred by Joseph Swartz in France. It was voted the 'best white climber' in 1908 by the National Rose Society of England. After his death, Swartz's widow went on to develop roses, including Mme Ernst Calvat and Roger Lambelin.

New Dawn

New Dawn is one of the all-time favorite climbing varieties among gardeners and rosarians. Dr. William Van Fleet of the U.S. originally introduced the hybrid seedling in 1910. In the 1920s, a repeat-blooming sport was introduced as The New Dawn. During the 1997 Triennial Convention in Benelux, members of the World Federation of Rose Societies elected New Dawn into the Hall of Fame. It was celebrated as the first patented plant in the world.

Other names:
Everblooming Dr. W. Van Fleet, The New Dawn

Flower color:
pale pearl pink

Flower size: 3–3½" (7.6–9 cm)

Scent: sweet and fresh, apple

Height: 15–20' (4.5–6.1 m)

Spread: 10–15' (3–4.5 m)

Blooms: early summer to fall; repeat blooming

Hardiness zones: 4–9

❀ New Dawn is known for its double flowers that fade from a soft pink to a more pinkish white. The blossoms are borne both in small clusters and singly. It bears plentiful, shiny foliage on upright arching canes. The foliage is mildly prone to mildew on the tips of the stems later in the season but otherwise is disease resistant.

❀ Considered one of the easiest climbers to grow, this rose is suitable for pergolas, walls, fences, arches or pillars or can be pruned as a hedge or shrub. It is also a good rose for exhibition. It tolerates growing on a north-facing wall.

Royal Sunset

Royal Sunset bears an abundance of dense, leathery, dark green foliage. The bronze and copper foliar highlights complement the bright summery blossoms. Intense apricot orange blossoms fade to a soft pink, tinged with apricot hues. It will bloom on new and old wood. The flowers, borne in clusters, are cupped, semi-double and look like hybrid tea blooms. It blooms profusely throughout summer well into fall.

✿ Most apricot-colored climbers have a leggy growth habit, but Royal Sunset does not. It produces bushy, stiff growth that is best suited to growing against walls or fences or in a large area where it can be fanned out onto a support.

✿ Heavy reddish canes and attractive hips will provide color well into winter in milder climates.

✿ The plant requires winter protection in areas and microclimates colder than zone 5. A mulch of straw or wood shavings works well to insulate the plant.

Other names: none
Flower color: apricot pink with blended yellow
Flower size: 4½–5" (11–13 cm)
Scent: strong and fruity
Height: 6–10' (1.8–3 m)
Spread: 6' (1.8 m)
Blooms: mid-season; repeat blooming
Hardiness zones: 5–10

Royal Sunset was awarded the Portland Gold Medal in 1960, the year it was introduced.

Seagull

S eagull was developed in 1907 by Pritchard of the U.K. This white rambler bears vigorous arching canes that support large clusters of single and semi-double white flowers. The cupped flowers are intensely fragrant and expose gold stamens among the pure white petals. The foliage is dense, bearing gray-green pointed leaflets.

Other names: none
Flower color: white
Flower size: 1½" (3.8 cm)
Scent: sweet and strong
Height: 20' (6.1 m)
Spread: 12' (3.6 m)
Blooms: mid-summer; no repeat blooming
Hardiness zones: 4–9

❁ This variety is excellent for training on arches, pergolas, fences, walls, embankments or sturdy trellises.
❁ Seagull is very effective twining up an old tree with a bench at the base for an all-out display.
❁ Considered one of the best white modern, rambling roses available, Seagull won the Royal Horticultural Society Award of Garden Merit in 1993.

With its dense flower clusters, this is a rose for those who like a fuller effect.

Sombreuil

S ombreuil is the oldest climbing hybrid tea rose. It was introduced in 1851 in France and typifies the classic old rose style. It bears large, white, double, somewhat muddled flowers that occasionally display a touch of pink and yellow. The refined quilled petals open flat into quartered, doubled blossoms. Each flower consists of 100 petals, and the blooms blend beautifully with the semi-glossy, medium green leaves on purplish green, moderately thorny canes.

✿ This rose is suitable for climbing pillars, trellises, arbors, old trees and pergolas. It is easy to grow and resistant to rust and blackspot. It benefits from a location in full sun and tends to lose a little of its form and size in a shady spot.

✿ Deadheading, thinning, removing dead canes and light pruning will improve the flowering performance, growth habit and vigor.

Other names: Colonial White, Mlle de Sombreuil

Flower color: white

Flower size: 3½–4" (9–10 cm)

Scent: sweet green apple

Height: 12–15' (3.6–4.5 m)

Spread: 6–8' (1.8–2.4 m)

Blooms: mid-season; repeat blooming

Hardiness zones: 6–9

This rose was named after Mademoiselle de Sombreuil, a heroine from the French Revolution.

Veilchenblau

Other names: Blue Rambler, Violet Blue, Blue Rosalie

Flower color: soft reddish violet

Flower size: 1–1½" (2.5–3.8 cm)

Scent: light green apple

Height: 12–15' (3.6–4.5 m)

Spread: 8–12' (2.4–3.6 m)

Blooms: spring; no repeat blooming

Hardiness zones: 4–9

Veilchenblau is German for 'violet-blue,' a reference to the color of the blossoms. The flowers are not a true blue but appear more blue when grown in partial shade. The blue is further enhanced as the blooms fade with age and take on a gray-blue cast.

❀ Veilchenblau is a small-flowered rambler with loose clusters of semi-double, violet blooms with white streaks. The flowers have have a subtle fruity scent and are complemented by fine, sharply pointed, glossy, medium green leaves on arching, almost thornless canes.

❀ Generally disease resistant, this rose can suffer blackspot and mildew when planted where air circulation is poor or where drafts occur.

This vigorous rose is most attractive when twining through an old, sturdy tree in an informal setting.

Warm Welcome

E asy and reliable sums up Warm Welcome, a rose that is easy to grow and train and highly disease and weather resistant. It produces upright, arching, stiff canes well clothed in dark, semi-glossy leaves. The young foliage is inclined to darken with age from a purplish shade to a deep bronzy green. This rose bears semi-double clusters of small, deep orange flowers that contrast well with the foliage.

Other names: none
Flower color:
orange; yellow centers
Flower size: 2" (5 cm)
Scent: slight
Height: 7–8' (2.1–2.4 m)
Spread: 7' (2.1 m)
Blooms: summer to fall; repeat blooming
Hardiness zones: 4–9

✿ This climbing miniature rose can be trained to grow up walls, fences, trellises or pillars but is most appropriate for confined spaces.

✿ Warm Welcome is covered with blossoms throughout the season and considered healthier than most other readily available miniature varieties. Deadheading isn't necessary, and attractive hips form throughout fall into winter.

✿ This rose has won several awards including the Royal National Rose Society Presidents' International Trophy in 1988.

The creation of Warm Welcome was regarded as a hybridizing breakthrough because the free-blooming habit was retained.

HYBRID TEA

The first hybrid teas were bred around 1867, a turning point for roses. With the introduction of these roses, the era of old garden roses ended and the era of modern roses began. Hybrid teas are the dominant roses in the cut-flower industry and the garden. They are upright bushes with strong, prickly canes and usually have one flower per cane. Hybrid teas bloom continually throughout the growing season until a hard fall frost. The flowers are large, double blooms with a pointed form and an extensive color range, including all colors except blue, black and green. Some varieties are intensely fragrant.

Hybrid teas need winter protection in colder areas and are somewhat prone to blackspot. Use hybrid teas in a formal rose garden or cut-flower garden, in borders or as specimens. Hybrid teas can also be grown in containers although they will require further care and protection to get them successfully through the winter.

Barbra Streisand

An avid gardener, Barbra Streisand approached Tom Carruth of Weeks Roses in 1996 and asked him to create a rose for her. He chose three seedlings for her to try, and nine months later she chose this rose. It is fragrant, naturally vigorous and disease resistant and is now featured in the singer's Malibu rose garden, which contains over 1200 roses. It bears sprays of highly fragrant lavender blossoms. The petal edges are somewhat darker, and the depth of the color at the edge of the petals changes depending on the time of year. Each fully double flower is made up of 35 or more petals atop deep green, glossy foliage. This dusty mauve-pink rose has all the qualities one could want from a modern hybrid tea and is destined to become a classic.

Other names: none

Flower color: pinkish lavender

Flower size: 4–5" (10–13 cm)

Scent: old rose and citrus

Height: 3–4' (91–122 cm)

Spread: 24–36" (61–91 cm)

Blooms: summer to fall; repeat blooming

Hardiness zones: 5–9

❀ This rose is fairly upright and bushy. It may need a little pruning every couple of years to encourage a dense growth habit. It is a healthy rose for its color class but not completely disease free. Take the necessary precautions to prevent disease.

❀ Although this rose blooms prolifically throughout the growing season, deadheading will further extend flowering.

❀ Flower color and mature size are best in locations with milder temperatures. This rose tolerates high winds and salt air so is good for a coastal garden.

The flowers are borne on long, straight stems, allowing for fantastic cut flowers that last longer than most lavender-colored rose blooms.

Chicago Peace

Chicago Peace is a sport of the Peace rose and has the overall appearance of its parent but in a more spectacular color range. The yellow-based petals are touched with deep pink, copper and soft orange. This rose bears large, colorful, evenly spaced flowers atop dark, leathery foliage on moderately thorny, sturdy branches.

❀ Each flower is made up of 45–60 petals. The flower color fades with age to a softer palette yet remains stunning until the petals fall freely to the ground.

❀ Upright and vigorous, Chicago Peace is resistant to all common rose diseases except blackspot. Blackspot is less likely when the rose is planted in full sun.

❀ Prune each spring to reshape the shrub. Follow the technique used for pruning floribundas— prune the shrub down to the best five to seven buds on the best five to seven canes before the bud breaks.

Other names: none

Flower color: yellow, pink and apricot blend

Flower size: 6" (15 cm)

Scent: mild, fruity

Height: 4½–6½' (1.4–2 m)

Spread: 3–4' (91–122 cm)

Blooms: spring to later summer; repeat blooming

Hardiness zones: 4–9

This rose was discovered as a sport by a gardener named Johnston in Chicago, Illinois. It was entered into cultivation and introduced to the public for sale by the Conard-Pyle Company in 1962.

Dainty Bess

Other names:
The Artistic Rose

Flower color: pale pink

Flower size: 3½–4"
(9–10 cm)

Scent: light tea

Height: 24–30"
(61–76 cm)

Spread: 24" (61 cm)

Blooms: summer to first
frost; repeat blooming

Hardiness zones: 6–9

D ainty Bess, named after the hybridizer's wife, is still as popular and beautiful as it was when it was first introduced in 1925. Its single, ruffled, light pink flowers make it one of the most unusual hybrid tea varieties available. Rose stamens are usually yellow, but there is a 10 percent chance they will be burgundy. Dainty Bess is one of these rarities. The flowers are produced either singly or in clusters on very thorny, sturdy canes. When Dainty Bess is in flower, it truly is one of the most beautiful roses you could ever imagine.

✿ This rose isn't ideal for cutting, as the flowers are short-lived and the plant is so compact.

✿ The blossoms of this variety close at night, which is very unusual for roses.

✿ A climbing form of Dainty Bess is available today, with blooms similar to those of the original shrub form.

Among other awards, Dainty Bess received the 1925 Royal National Rose Society Gold Medal.

Double Delight

Double Delight is aptly named, as it delights with its strong, sweet fragrance as well as its unique flower color. The only drawback is the plant will very likely experience mildew or blackspot or both. But don't let that stop you, because it is one of the most popular roses available and worth growing for the fragrance alone! The fully double, high-centered flowers open cream with red edges and gradually darken to solid red. The color prompted the French to name this variety *La Rose de Rouge á Lévres*, 'The Lipstick Rose.'

Other names: Andeli

Flower color: cream; carmine red edges

Flower size: 5–5½" (13–14 cm)

Scent: strong, sweet with hint of spice

Height: 3–4' (91–122 cm)

Spread: 24–36" (61–91 cm)

Blooms: summer to fall; repeat blooming

Hardiness zones: 6–9

Double Delight is a long-lasting cut flower, a good choice for competition and exhibition.

✿ The unique color makes this beauty hard to place in a bed or border, so it is better used as a specimen. It is also suitable for containers, where it can be easily monitored for disease.

✿ A 1977 All-America Selection, Double Delight is suitable for a greenhouse or a warm, dry location. Keep this variety in full sun for the best color contrast. Rain doesn't seem to affect the blooms, but cool, wet weather can promote mildew. Blackspot can also be a problem.

✿ No two flowers are alike. Heat intensifies the bloom color while in cooler temperatures the color becomes more subtle. The award-winning fragrance is unaffected by temperature, light or age.

Elina

Other names: Peaudouce
Flower color: ivory white; yellow centers
Flower size: 5½–6" (14–15 cm)
Scent: very light
Height: 3–5' (91 cm–1.5 m)
Spread: 3' (91 cm)
Blooms: summer to frost; repeat blooming
Hardiness zones: 6–9

This rose used to be known as Peaudouce, French for 'soft skin.' The name was changed after a brand of infant diapers of the same name was introduced.

Elina is one of the best of its color and class. It is the perfect rose for the beginner to use as an exhibition variety, and its long stems make it a great cut flower. Slightly delayed flowering extends the bloom season. The blooms are evenly petaled, double and high centered. The bushy foliage has large, dark, slightly red-tinted leaves.

✿ While many light-colored blooms get mottled or spotty after rain, the flowers of this variety stand up well in rain.

✿ Elina is regarded as one of the most reliable and free-blooming hybrid teas available. It is almost always in bloom and boasts huge blossoms.

✿ In 1987, Elina was named the Anerkannte Deutsche Rose and received the New Zealand (Gold Star) Gold Medal; in 1994 it was awarded the James Mason Gold Medal.

✿ It boasts outstanding vigor, form and resistance to disease.

Fragrant Cloud

Although the full, bright red flowers are beautiful in their own right, Fragrant Cloud is known for its outstanding, unique fragrance. It has won seven awards for its beauty and fragrance, including the Gamble Fragrance Award in 1970. It is considered by the ARS to be one of the top 10 fragrant roses, which is a great accomplishment for a hybrid tea that was introduced only in 1963. The World Federation of Rose Societies' Hall of Fame rated it third best of all time. In a 1998 survey conducted by the CRS, Canadian rose growers rated Fragrant Cloud the second best fragrant rose.

Other names:
Nuage Parfume
Flower color:
orangy red
Flower size: 5" (13 cm)
Scent: intense and strong
Height: 4–5'
(1.2–1.5 m)
Spread: 32–36"
(81–91 cm)
Blooms: spring to fall;
repeat blooming
Hardiness zones: 5–9

Fragrant Cloud has been showered with numerous honors and awards, most in recognition of its outstanding scent.

❀ Fragrant Cloud has a bushy and upright growth habit, with well-branched canes that support glossy, dark green foliage. Typical to hybrid tea form, the full and evenly petaled flowers are high centered, double and made up of more than 30 petals each.

❀ It is ideal for borders and beds, requiring very little maintenance other than seasonal deadheading and a little spring pruning.

❀ Fragrant Cloud is only mildly prone to mildew in the fall and blackspot in damp weather.

❀ With its low-growing habit and tendency for fading flower color, Fragrant Cloud doesn't rank as one of the best cut-flower varieties.

❀ It tends to maintain the best flower color in cooler climates.

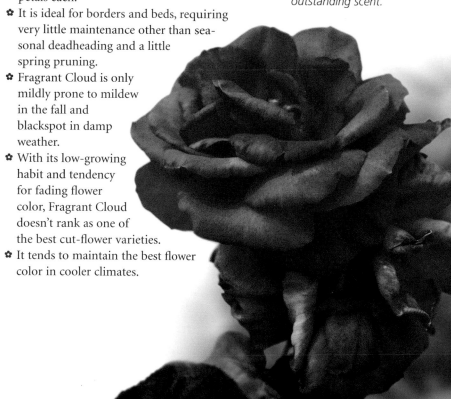

Garden Party

Other names: none

Flower color: cream; pale pink edges

Flower size: 4–5" (10–13 cm)

Scent: pleasant and light

Height: 4–5' (1.2–1.5 m)

Spread: 24–36" (61–91 cm)

Blooms: summer to fall; repeat blooming

Hardiness zones: 5–9

Garden Party was introduced in 1959 by Herbert C. Swim of the U.S. He wanted a rose that would not be damaged in the hot sun and that would bear petals that would fall cleanly from the plant.

Garden Party is delicate and soft in appearance. Beautiful urn-shaped buds open into graceful, fully double flowers. Each bloom consists of 25–30 long petals that form into a high-centered blossom and then become wavy as they reflex. The clusters of flowers are borne on the tips of upright stems, and the large, dark, semi-glossy leaves with reddish undersides offset the lovely flowers. The creamy soft yellow centers change to a soft pink towards the edges. Garden Party received the Bagatelle Gold Medal in 1959 and was an All-America Selection the following year.

✿ The beautifully constructed flowers first emerge freely in mid-season, taper off gradually and then bloom profusely later in the season. The flower color is most intense in the late-season flush.

✿ Garden Party bears most flowers when grown in full sun. Choose a location that provides enough sun for prolific blooming but doesn't cause the flower color to fade too quickly. This rose is ideal for cutting gardens, beds and containers. The cool shades are soothing among more brightly hued flowers and roses.

✿ This rose is highly resistant to blackspot but is a little prone to powdery mildew.

Gerda Hnatyshyn

Gerda Hnatyshyn bears perfect hybrid tea flowers in medium pink shades. The flowers are a little slow to open but well worth the wait. The attractive foliage creates a mass of dark green, thick, glossy leaves. With its long stems and long-lasting, sweetly fragrant blossoms, this is an excellent cut flower.

✿ Unlike most hybrid teas, this rose grows very well on its own roots. It is an early bloomer and continues to produce well into fall.

✿ This rose has excellent health and requires little care. It prefers rich soil and partial to full sun.

✿ Gerda Hnatyshyn is the wife of Ray Hnatyshyn, former governor general of Canada. In 1992, to celebrate the 125th anniversary of Canada's confederation, the Hnatyshyns launched an initiative for the design of the heritage rose gardens at Rideau Hall in Ottawa. The Hnatyshyns were in attendance with the current governor general, The Right Honourable Adrienne Clarkson, when the heritage rose garden was opened to the public in 2000.

Other names: none
Flower color: medium pink
Flower size: 4–5" (10–13 cm)
Scent: strong damask
Height: 4' (1.2 m)
Spread: 30" (76 cm)
Blooms: early summer to fall; repeat blooming
Hardiness zone: 4

This 2000 introduction was the first hybrid tea developed by Brad Jalbert of Select Roses.

Honor

Other names:
Honour, Michele Torr
Flower color: white
Flower size: 4–5"
(10–13 cm)
Scent: light
Height: 5–5½'
(1.5–1.6 m)
Spread: 4–5' (1.2–1.5 m)
Blooms: late spring to fall;
repeat blooming
Hardiness zones: 5–9

Honor was introduced in 1980 as part of the All American Series along with two other roses, Love (p. 243) and Cherish. Honor clearly has exhibition quality, winning the Portland Gold Medal in 1978 and the All-America Selection in 1980. This rose has a tall, upright and vigorous growth habit and bears satiny white buds that open to large blossoms with golden stamens. The flowers bloom in clusters or singly on long, moderately thorny canes and are suitable for cutting and arrangements. Each flower has 25–30 clear, velvety petals.

❀ Honor is a tender rose in cooler climates, so winter protection may be necessary.

❀ This rose produces long, strong stems ideal for cutting. To extend the vase life of the flowers, cut the stems when the blooms are in bud.

❀ Honor is perfectly suited to mixed borders and beds or works well as a stunning specimen. White-flowered roses stand out among just about any color grouping, especially when planted in large groups.

You don't have to be a rose aficionado to successfully grow this variety, as it is highly disease resistant and easy to maintain.

Ingrid Bergman

I ngrid Bergman is considered one of the best red-flowering hybrid teas for cutting. It is also extremely easy to grow. It is valued as one of the most dependable, dark red garden roses available. The flowers are borne in clear red, and the velvety petals hold their color very well. Long stems bear semi-glossy, deep green foliage.

✿ This hybrid tea is perfect as a standard for containers or borders.

✿ Generally very disease resistant, this rose is somewhat prone to blackspot.

✿ This rose has done extremely well in worldwide rose trials, proving over and over again that it would be an ideal addition to just about any garden setting. Similar to other Poulsen-bred roses, Ingrid Bergman is adaptable and versatile and is as poplar now as it was when it was introduced in 1984.

Other names: none
Flower color: crimson red
Flower size: 4½" (11 cm)
Scent: very light
Height: 3–3½'
(91–107 cm)
Spread: 24–30"
(61–76 cm)
Blooms: summer to fall; repeat blooming
Hardiness zones: 5–9

Developed in Denmark and named after the Hollywood actress, Ingrid Bergman was one of the most highly acclaimed roses of the 1980s. In 2000 it was chosen as the World's Favorite Rose by the World Federation of Rose Societies.

Liebeszauber

L iebeszauber is a vigorous rose with an upright growth habit. The foliage emerges red in early spring and matures to a deep, dark green. The pure dark red blossoms are loosely cupped, wavy-petaled and sweetly fragrant.

Other names:
Crimson Spire

Flower color: dark red

Flower size: 6–7"
(15–18 cm)

Scent: very sweet

Height: 3½–6'
(1.1–1.8 m)

Spread: 3½' (1.1 m)

Blooms: summer to fall; repeat blooming

Hardiness zones: 5–9

✿ The strong stems are suitable for cutting or training. This rose would be ideal for exhibiting at a rose show or for display planting in a mixed border. It is best planted at the back of borders because it is so vigorous—the occasional shoot reaches heights of 6½' (2 m) by fall if left intact.

✿ This hybrid tea blooms like a floribunda, bearing its flowers singly and in clusters that stand up well in the rain.

✿ Liebeszauber has a tendency to send up spindly canes occasionally, but these are easily removed with a quick snip. A more manageable, balanced bush can be trained by pinching out the side buds. This rose requires a hard prune each year.

The name of this rose is German for 'love's magic.'

Loving Memory

Loving Memory is one of the best red hybrid tea roses. It grows in a symmetrical form, producing very long stems with high-centered, deep red blooms. The large, long-lasting blooms are fully double and packed with 40 or more petals each. Loving Memory is a robust variety with a bushy, upright growth habit. It is great as an exhibition rose and for large borders or along the back of shrub or perennial beds.

Other names: Red Cedar, Burgund 81, Kordes' Rose Burgund
Flower color: deep red
Flower size: 5" (13 cm)
Scent: sweet yet subtle
Height: 3½' (1.1 m)
Spread: 30" (76 cm)
Blooms: spring to fall; repeat blooming
Hardiness zones: 5–10

✿ This rose blooms freely throughout most of the growing season and is moderately disease resistant. The dark, semi-glossy foliage suffers little mildew or blackspot.

✿ Different countries have used different names for this rose. It is known as Red Cedar in Australia; Loving Memory in the U.K., Canada and New Zealand; and Burgund 81 in Germany.

Peace

Other names: Gloria Dei, Mme A. Meilland, Gioia, Beke, Fredsrosen

Flower color: soft yellow; baby pink edges

Flower size: 5½–6" (14–15 cm)

Scent: mild and fruity

Height: 5½–6½' (1.5–2 m)

Spread: 3½–4' (1.1–1.2 m)

Blooms: summer to fall; repeat blooming

Hardiness zones: 5–9

This rose was originally named after the breeder's mother, Claudia, but was renamed in the United States to celebrate the end of World War II and to promote world peace.

Peace has been referred to as the Rose of the Century, which is a lot to live up to, but this rose is more than capable. It is very easy to grow and one of the most famous roses ever produced. It has won many awards including the All-America Selection in 1946. It is an upright grower with moderately thorny canes and large, glossy foliage. Even out of bloom, this shrub looks great. The yellow can become pale if the location is too hot, while the pink intensifies in heat.

❀ Peace is an ideal cut-flower variety. It is suitable for rose beds, hedges and borders. It is considered one of the best varieties to grow as a standard. It is a little resentful of hard pruning but fares well with moderate pruning.

❀ Climbing Peace is a sport of Peace that can reach heights of 15–20' (4.6–6.1 m).

❀ Peace has a moderate level of disease resistance but is prone to blackspot in cooler climates. Its overall health has been compromised as a result of being cloned millions of times since its introduction in 1945.

❀ Peace, the first rose to be selected World's Favorite Rose by the World Federation of Rose Societies, received that honor in 1976.

Rosemary Harkness

Rosemary Harkness is often the first rose to bloom in late spring or early summer. It bears delicate apricot- and pink-edged flowers followed by abundant glossy, dark green foliage. The marbled flower color is a stunning, eye-catching combination of tones and shades.

❁ This vigorous, spreading variety is ideal as a garden feature or specimen. It also blends easily into a mixed bed or border, but leave enough space for it to reach its mature size.

❁ Rosemary Harkness doesn't mind being trimmed and trained into topiary, a hedge or a standard. It is highly disease resistant and easy to grow.

❁ Rose gardeners seek out this plant for its scent—it is one of the most scented modern roses.

Other names: none

Flower color: apricot yellow; salmon pink edges

Flower size: 4" (10 cm)

Scent: sweet, like passionfruit

Height: 30" (76 cm)

Spread: 30" (76 cm)

Blooms: late spring to fall; repeat blooming

Hardiness zones: 5–9

Rosemary Harkness was raised in England by Harkness in 1985. It was named after the niece of the late Jack Harkness, former rose breeder of Harkness Roses.

Royal William

Other names: Duftzauber '84, Fragrant Charm 84, Leonora Christine

Flower color: deep, velvety crimson red

Flower size: 5" (13 cm)

Scent: spicy and sweet but strong

Height: 3' (91 cm)

Spread: 30" (76 cm)

Blooms: mid-summer to fall; repeat blooming

Hardiness zones: 5–9

Royal William has an exceptional sweet and spicy fragrance and noble beauty. It bears velvety red flowers accompanied by dark green, semi-glossy foliage.

✿ Royal William is a perfect rose for the avid rose-show participant and the average gardener alike. It can be used in mixed beds and borders, in containers or as specimens.

✿ This vigorous, disease-resistant rose is frequently used as a cut flower.

✿ Royal William was developed in Germany in 1984 by Kordes. It has won many awards, including the Royal Horticultural Society Award of Garden Merit in 1993 and Rose of the Year in 1987.

Savoy Hotel

Savoy Hotel is a vigorous, bushy shrub with dark green, glossy foliage. It has a prolonged blooming period in late spring to early summer. The fully double high-centered form is superb. The undersides of the flower petals are slightly darker pink than the uppersides.

❀ The long-lasting blooms lend themselves well to cutting for a variety of floral arrangements.

❀ This rose is a good exhibition rose and works well in borders or beds or as a standard. It performs well in cool summers and can handle some cooler winter temperatures.

❀ The flowers will not open during extended rainy periods.

Other names: Integrity
Flower color: light pink
Flower size: 4–6"
(10–15 cm)
Scent: none
Height: 3–4' (91–122 cm)
Spread: 24" (61 cm)
Blooms: late spring to fall; repeat blooming
Hardiness zones: 5–9

Savoy Hotel was bred by Harkness in England in 1987 from Silver Jubilee and Amber Queen. It was named to mark the centennial of the Savoy Hotel in London, England.

Selfridges

This vigorous, disease-resistant hybrid tea bears well-shaped yellow flowers on very long stems. The yellow intensifies when the blooms are fully open. The flowers tend to fade quickly, especially after a rainfall. Glossy, deep green foliage covers the stems from top to bottom. Selfridges produces large canes that develop each year from the ground up but begin blooming only in the second year.

Other names: Berolina
Flower color: yellow
Flower size: 3–4"
(7.6–10 cm)
Scent: strong tea
Height: up to 7' (2.1 m)
Spread: 4–5' (1.2–1.5 m)
Blooms: spring to fall;
repeat blooming
Hardiness zones: 5–9

✿ This rose was introduced in 1984 by Kordes, so it will likely be a successful rose. It is quickly developing a great reputation as one of the best yellow hybrid teas available in a coastal environment.

✿ With its ability to grow so high, Selfridges is well suited to the back of a mixed bed or border. It can be trained as a climber on a trellis or arbor.

✿ It was named to honor the 75th anniversary of the famous London department store Selfridges.

Warm Wishes

This All-America Selection was named Warm Wishes when it was introduced to the American market, but the name was changed in 1998 to Sunset Celebration to commemorate the 10th anniversary of *Sunset* magazine. Though many rose gardeners still call it Warm Wishes, its new name is appropriate because the rose exhibits almost every color of a Pacific Northwest sunset. This evenly balanced bush bears large, fully double flowers made up of an average of 30 or more petals each. The long, elegant buds open up to a classic, high-centered spiral. The well-formed flowers are borne singly or in clusters atop dark, glossy foliage.

Other names:
Sunset Celebration, Chantoli, Exotic
Flower color:
soft peachy coral
Flower size: 4½–5½" (11–14 cm)
Scent: sweet and fruity
Height: 3–5' (91 cm–1.5 m)
Spread: 24–30" (61–76 cm)
Blooms: summer to fall; repeat blooming
Hardiness zones: 4–9

✿ The flower color changes over time and varies depending on heat and moisture. It sometimes evolves from apricot or amber to a subtle shade of pink with peach tones.

✿ The long-stemmed, colorful blooms are ideal for cutting, and the cut flowers last seven days or more.

✿ Warm Wishes makes an impact planted en masse or as a specimen. It works well in mixed beds and borders and thrives in a container.

This hybrid tea is establishing itself as one of the finest introductions of recent years and has received a number of awards.

FLORIBUNDA

Floribundas are upright to free-branching bushes with prickly canes. The class was produced by crossing hybrid teas with polyanthas. They are generally smaller plants than the hybrid teas, but have the same color range and hardiness. The clusters or sprays of small flowers bloom abundantly throughout the growing season, often smothering the foliage with blossoms. They often lack the flower form of the hybrid teas, but continued hybridization is improving the flower form. Use a floribunda in a bed or border, as a specimen, in a container or as a hedge.

Polyanthas, produced from crossing *Rosa multiflora* with *Rosa chinensis*, are the forerunners to the floribundas. Polyanthas are compact, free-branching bushes with sparsely prickly stems. They are hardier than floribundas. Polyantha is Latin for 'many flowers,' and these roses do flower profusely in clusters. There are few polyantha varieties left in commerce as they have been superseded by the floribundas.

Ainsley Dickson

Other names: Dicky, Dickimono, Munchner Kindl

Flower color: salmon pink

Flower size: 3–3½" (7.6–9 cm)

Scent: light and sweet

Height: 3' (91 cm)

Spread: 30" (76 cm)

Blooms: summer to early fall; repeat blooming

Hardiness zones: 4–9

This rose was named after the wife of the rose's creator.

Ainsley Dickson has many outstanding qualities, including the long-pointed buds that open to evenly petaled, salmon pink flowers that virtually cover the plant. Each flower consists of 35 petals in a high-centered form, and each petal is slightly darker on the top and paler underneath. Dark, glossy foliage covers the moderately thorny stems.

❀ Introduced in 1983, Ainsley Dickson is a fair representation of the bloom and growth habits of the floribundas from that time. It has won numerous awards over the past two decades, including the Royal Horticultural Society Award of Garden Merit in 1993.

❀ This rose is ideal for borders, beds or containers. It is also a good exhibition rose. It requires very little maintenance and is highly disease resistant. On the coast it may experience a little powdery mildew.

❀ Ainsley Dickson can bear up to 120 blooms in its first year. It has a reliable repeat bloom later in the season if located in full sun.

City of London

When left alone, City of London has a spreading and uneven growth habit. It bears small clusters of loosely double, pale pink blossoms noted for their everlasting fragrance. The urn-shaped blossoms become flat over time but hold their color. In early spring an abundance of dark, glossy foliage is borne. The foliage is highly disease resistant, but on the coast, prevention and monitoring may be necessary to curb the potential for blackspot.

✿ With its profuse blooming habit, City of London consistently replaces the spent individual blooms, especially after a rainfall.

✿ The almost thornless canes of City of London can be trained to grow up arbors, trellises and pergolas. The plant can be gently pruned into a rounded shrub. The flowers blend beautifully when combined with old garden rose varieties. It is an excellent rose for cut-flower gardens, beds or borders or for showing.

✿ City of London won the New Zealand Fragrance Award in 1992 and both the Royal Horticultural Society Award of Garden Merit and The Hague Gold Medal in 1993.

Other names: none
Flower color: pearl pink
Flower size: 3" (7.6 cm)
Scent: sweet, powerful and long lasting
Height: 4–6' (1.2–1.8 m)
Spread: 30"–4' (76–122 cm)
Blooms: summer to fall; repeat blooming
Hardiness zones: 4–9

This rose was named to commemorate the 800th anniversary of London's charter and was introduced by Harkness of England in 1988.

Easy Going

Easy Going is a sport of Fellowship, an orange floribunda (p. 229), and has all the fine attributes of its parent. It is well known for its reliable vigor, attractive foliage and long-lasting, colorful blossoms. It bears large, cupped blooms of 30–40 petals each. The flowers are produced in large clusters atop a rounded growth habit. The dark, glossy foliage is especially resistant to blackspot and other typical problems that roses encounter.

Other names: none
Flower color: amber yellow
Flower size: 4½" (11 cm)
Scent: pleasant and fruity
Height: 3–3½' (91–107 cm)
Spread: 24–30" (61–76 cm)
Blooms: summer to fall; repeat blooming
Hardiness zones: 5–9

✿ Easy Going is most effective in group plantings. The golden flowers stand out when planted in a formal border. It is also a great cut flower.
✿ This vigorous rose is easy to maintain.
✿ Easy Going was introduced by Harkness of the U.K. in 1996.

Escapade

Escapade is a sturdy and reliable rose. It is disease and weather resistant and responds well to the occasional hard prune. The flowers can fade to a lilac pink in cooler locations or pale pink in hot areas. The saucer-shaped blooms are borne in clusters of well-spaced sprays among glossy leaves on moderately thorny canes.

❀ With its long-lasting, dainty and wild-looking blooms, Escapade deserves to be more widely grown. The flowers are ideal for cutting, especially when cut in bud.

❀ This semi-double floribunda rose is simple and unobtrusive in a typical landscape setting. It blends well in herbaceous borders and cutting gardens and is dense enough for hedging. It is ideal for showing.

Other names: none

Flower color: deep violet pink; white centers

Flower size: 3" (7.6 cm)

Scent: lightly sweet and spicy

Height: 30–36" (76–91 cm)

Spread: 24" (61 cm)

Blooms: summer to fall; repeat blooming

Hardiness zones: 5–9

Since its 1967 introduction, Escapade has won several awards in Baden-Baden, Erfurt and Belfast, and it has received prizes in Copenhagen, proving that even a modest rose won't go unnoticed.

Eyepaint

E yepaint bears single red flowers with white centers that appear hand painted. Each flower has an average of five to six petals. Eyepaint vigorously performs like a bushy shrub rose. It has an abundance of small, dark foliage and very thorny canes. It is ideal for hedging, group plantings and along the back of borders.

Other names:
Eye Paint, Tapis Persan
Flower color:
red; white centers
Flower size: 2½" (6.4 cm)
Scent: delicate
Height: 3–4'
(91–122 cm)
Spread: 30" (76 cm)
Blooms: summer to fall; repeat blooming
Hardiness zones: 5–9

❁ With a little pruning and training, Eyepaint can be allowed to grow very tall and create a pillar-like appearance.

❁ Eyepaint is sure to make an impact, becoming even more prolific when deadheaded. Deadhead when the entire truss is at least 85 percent spent.

❁ This relatively hardy rose tolerates extreme weather. It is a little sensitive to drought, prone to blackspot and requires some deadheading to keep it looking its best. Still, it is generally disease resistant and easily trained.

❁ It received the Royal National Rose Society Trial Ground Certificate in 1973, was introduced to the public in 1976 and won the 1978 Belfast Gold Medal.

The name was apparently a nickname that turned out to be the perfect name after all.

Fellowship

People love a rose that's rarely out of bloom, and this is one such rose. Fellowship produces well-formed buds followed by glowing blooms that retain their color very well. This rose is strong in its color class, dense and spreading in form. Its glossy foliage is a solid base to the fully open flowers with their showy yellow stamens. It is ideal in beds or mass plantings or as a cut flower or exhibition rose.

✿ Fellowship won the Royal National Rose Society Gold Medal in 1990 and was the All-America Selection in 1996.

✿ Fellowship lives up to another name it is known by—Livin' Easy. The beautiful foliage is highly disease resistant. This is one of the healthiest roses ever grown at Select Roses in B.C.

Many of these roses showcase pathways in London's Regents Park. Fellowship has been well used in home gardens as well.

Other names: Livin' Easy
Flower color: fiery apricot orange blend
Flower size: 3–4" (7.6–10 cm)
Scent: fruity and sweet
Height: 3–4' (91–122 cm)
Spread: 3' (91 cm)
Blooms: summer to fall; repeat blooming
Hardiness zones: 5–9

Friesia

Other names: Sunsprite
Flower color:
bright lemon yellow
Flower size: 3" (7.6 cm)
Scent: sweet licorice
Height: 30–36"
(76–91 cm)
Spread: 24" (61 cm)
Blooms: mid-season
to fall; repeat blooming
Hardiness zones: 5–11

Friesia is one of the best yellow floribunda roses, not only for color and habit but for fragrance as well. It was the winner of an award in Baden-Baden in part for its outstanding scent. The flowers maintain long-lasting color without fading. The glossy foliage becomes stocky and compact over time.

✿ It is easily grown as a standard or as low, colorful hedging and is one of the best bedding roses available.
✿ Only minimal maintenance is required, including an annual prune and adequate mulching. Deadhead to keep the plant neat and tidy.
✿ This rose is disease resistant and vigorous.
✿ A new climbing form now available is best used on arbors and trellises.

Friesia was named after the province in Germany where it originated in 1977.

Glad Tidings

G lad Tidings was introduced in Tantau, Germany, in 1989 and rated one of the best floribundas created. It produces an abundance of glossy, dark green foliage and masses of showy clusters of velvety red flowers. Each flower consists of an average of 20 petals, resulting in cupped rosettes.

❀ This rose is suitable for beds, borders and exhibitions. The long-lasting blooms are perfect for cutting.

❀ It is fairly disease resistant, but a location with adequate air circulation will help prevent blackspot.

❀ There is little fragrance but the succession of blooms through summer and fall is great.

❀ The crimson blooms can withstand wet weather without becoming marked.

Other names: Lubecker Rotspon, Peter Wessel

Flower color: dark crimson red

Flower size: 2–3" (5–7.6 cm)

Scent: little to none

Height: 24–36" (61–91 cm)

Spread: 24" (61 cm)

Blooms: summer to fall; repeat blooming

Hardiness zones: 5–9

Iceberg

Over 40 years have passed since Reimer Kordes introduced this rose into commerce, and it has stood the test of time. The shapely, rain-resistant blooms last a long time and are ideal for cutting or left on the plant to adorn a special place in the garden. The buds emerge with a touch of pink and open into well-formed, dainty, white, semi-double flowers. Each flower is made up of 30–35 petals in clusters of up to 15 flowers.

Other names: Fée des Neiges, Schneewittchen
Flower color: white
Flower size: 3–4" (7.6–10 cm)
Scent: strong, sweet
Height: 3–4' (91–122 cm)
Spread: 3–4' (91–122 cm)
Blooms: early to mid-season; repeat blooming
Hardiness zones: 4–9

✿ The blooms tend to be flushed with pink when the nights are cold and damp, especially in early spring and fall. If dew or a raindrop remains on a petal in the morning, it may also activate the color change and turn the part of the petal that it touched pink.

✿ This sweetly fragrant rose is ideal in mixed beds or borders, planted in large groups or left alone as a specimen.

✿ A sport of Iceberg, Climbing Iceberg, is a climber easily trained on small fences, pergolas, arches, pillars and veranda posts. It is considered one of the best white climbing roses available, bearing disease-resistant foliage on almost thornless stems.

The lull between bloom cycles for this rose is very short, so it appears to be in bloom continually.

Lavaglow

L avaglow was developed in 1978 by Kordes. It bears camellia-like red flowers that are so dark they almost appear black. An average of 20–25 petals make up each velvety blossom. The evenly spaced clusters are well maintained through summer and fall. Glossy, purplish green leaves complement the ruffled, velvety flowers that last and last.

❁ Its balanced growth habit makes this an outstanding bedding variety. Other uses include mixed borders or hedging.

❁ Protection from blackspot may be required where damp weather is common.

❁ Dark red roses can often suffer scorch in heat and wind, but the blooms of Lavaglow do not suffer in hot sun, wind or rain.

❁ Lavaglow is sometimes confused with Intrigue, a rose bred by Warriner in 1982 that bears dark reddish purple flowers. Lavaglow is not always as readily available as the later-bred Intrigue, but it is well worth a search as it possesses great floribunda qualities.

Other names: Lavaglut
Flower color: dark red
Flower size: 3" (7.6 cm)
Scent: light tea
Height: 3–4' (91–122 cm)
Spread: 24" (61 cm)
Blooms: summer to fall; repeat blooming
Hardiness zones: 4–9

This rose was awarded the Royal National Rose Society Trial Ground Certificate in 1980.

Mountbatten

M ountbatten hasn't been widely known since its 1982 introduction but has won many awards. Before it was introduced to the public, it won the Lyon Rose of the Century in 1980. It is healthy, disease resistant and strong growing and a great choice for poor soil.

Other names: none
Flower color:
medium yellow
Flower size: 4" (10 cm)
Scent: sweet
Height: 3–5'
(91 cm–1.5 m)
Spread: 30" (76 cm)
Blooms: summer to fall;
repeat blooming
Hardiness zones: 5–10

✿ Neat round buds open to long-lasting, soft yellow blooms. The flowers are borne on tall stems that support an abundance of glossy, dark foliage. Each flower consists of 45 petals, resulting in a fully double form.

✿ This rose is ideal for hedging, borders and mixed beds and perfect as a standard. It can be trained as a specimen shrub with light pruning, which will reduce the overall height but maintain the dense, rounded growth habit.

✿ Mountbatten is very easy to grow and requires little care.

This Harkness-bred rose was named after the late Lord Mountbatten.

Pensioner's Voice

Pensioner's Voice won the National Rose Society Trial Ground Certificate in 1989. This rose is a little underused in home gardens but attracts a lot of attention wherever it's grown. It bears long, arching stems tipped with well-spaced flower clusters. The flowers, large for a floribunda, are reminiscent of hybrid tea blooms in form and substance. The petals reflex as the flowers open into the high-centered, cupped form. The flowers are deep apricot, often flushed with orangy red towards the edges of each petal.

Other names: Michelle Wright

Flower color: apricot pink

Flower size: 2½–3" (6–7.6 cm)

Scent: pleasant, fruity

Height: 3–5' (91 cm–1.5 m)

Spread: 24" (61 cm)

Blooms: summer to fall; repeat blooming

Hardiness zones: 4–9

❀ Pensioner's Voice is quick to repeat its blooming cycle, so it is useful as a cut flower in dry or fresh arrangements.

❀ This rose is highly disease resistant and extremely vigorous. The neatly formed flowers may be overwhelmed by younger shoots. Prune as you would any floribunda (see Pruning, in the Introduction).

❀ Pensioner's Voice is most effective in mass plantings or along the back of mixed borders—shorter plants in front will disguise its irregular, delicate growth habit. This rose is fantastic in beds in just about any setting.

Pensioner's Voice is also available as a standard, through specialty rose catalogs by mail order or via the internet. Most growers and rose retailers consider it one of the most popular and reliable roses.

Playboy

Playboy has been widely used in warmer climates because the intense flower color is enhanced by hot weather. Wavy-petaled flowers appear almost single, opening from clusters of pointed buds. Each blossom displays dazzling tones of yellow blended with shades of apricot and red and reveals beautiful bright yellow stamens. Moderately thorny canes support an abundance of dark, glossy leaves. The flowers are slightly cupped with an open form. Each semi-double flower consists of seven to ten petals, resulting in a typical floribunda form.

Other names: Cheerio
Flower color: yellowy orange; red edges
Flower size: 3½" (9 cm)
Scent: light apple scent
Height: 3' (91 cm)
Spread: 24" (61 m)
Blooms: summer to fall; repeat blooming
Hardiness zones: 5–9

✿ This rose truly lives up to its name, as it is smooth and charming in nature and appearance.
✿ Playboy is great for hedges, mixed beds and borders but is best suited to a location that's begging for bright colors. This vigorous, compact yet slightly upright rose lends a brilliant impact to any garden.
✿ It was introduced in 1976 by Cocker's Roses in Scotland and won the Portland Gold Medal in 1989, one of many honors it has received throughout the years.

When arranged with the right combination of flowers, Playboy packs a lot of punch as a cut flower.

Sexy Rexy

S exy Rexy blooms considerably later than most floribundas but bears a huge first flush of blooms. It requires very little maintenance or pruning. It has a well-branched form that is dense and upright, and the thorny canes bear small, glossy, dark green foliage. Camellia-like, pale pink flowers that bloom and last for weeks are borne on the stem tips. Each flower consists of 40 or more petals. The fragrance is reminiscent of tea—fresh and subtle.

✿ The beautifully formed flowers sometimes bow down almost to the ground after a heavy rain.
✿ Sexy Rexy will produce an abundance of blooms a second time around after summer deadheading and trimming. When pruning, reduce the stems by up to one-half their length.
✿ Versatile with exhibition qualities, this rose can be used in beds, borders, massed plantings, cutting gardens or containers. It can be grown as a standard.

*Sexy Rexy has received many
awards, including the RNRS James
Mason Gold Medal in 1996.
It blooms vigorously and is
easy to grow.*

Other names:
Heckenzauber
Flower color:
medium to light pink
Flower size: 3½–4"
(9–10 cm)
Scent: slight tea
Height: 3–4'
(91 cm–1.2 m)
Spread: 30–36"
(76–91 cm)
Blooms: late summer;
repeat blooming
Hardiness zones: 5–11

Sheila's Perfume

Other names: none

Flower color: pale yellow and light pink; dark pink edges

Flower size: 3½" (9 cm)

Scent: strong, rosy fruit

Height: 30"–3½' (76–107 cm)

Spread: 24" (61 cm)

Blooms: summer to fall; repeat blooming

Hardiness zones: 5–11

Its name is a combination of the name of the hybridizer's wife and its most outstanding quality, hence Sheila's Perfume.

Sheila's Perfume is a compact bush that tends to spread over summer in warmer climates. Showy bicolored blooms on short stems top red-tinted, glossy, dark green foliage. The double flowers are made up of an average of 20 petals each, borne singly or in clusters.

❀ This vigorous 1985 introduction is disease resistant and weatherproof. It was bred and raised by an amateur hybridizer named Sheridan in England and has achieved international popularity. The parentage of this rose is Peer Gynt x (Daily Sketch x [Paddy McGredy x Prima Ballerina]).

❀ Sheila's Perfume bears a classically formed flower, making this plant ideal for a cutting garden or for borders, hedges, mixed beds or containers.

❀ It has won several fragrance awards, including the Edland Fragrance Award in 1981 and the Glasgow Fragrance Award in 1989.

Tabris

Tabris blooms prolifically in its first year. By the second year, the flower production plateaus but the blooms maintain themselves for longer periods. Showy blooms top glossy, dark green foliage. Sprays of cupped, double flowers consist of 35 petals each. The foliage grows in plentiful mounds, a little open in habit and spreading in nature.

✿ This rose can be used in containers, cutting gardens, beds and borders. With its spreading thorny canes and growth habit, it can also work as a great barrier rose.

✿ Mostly weather resistant, Tabris is a little prone to blackspot. A warmer location helps prevent the disease and intensifies the flower color.

✿ Some people think that this is the same rose as Hannah Gordon and Nicole and that, though they have different registered names, they were all bred by the same breeder. The three appear to be almost identical, with subtle differences noticed only by keen eyes. Regardless of the confusion, if you find a specimen by any of these names, the overall coloration, growth habit and fragrance will be the same.

Other names: Hannah Gordon, Raspberry Ice, Nicole

Flower color: soft cream; raspberry red edges

Flower size: 3" (7.6 cm)

Scent: light and sweet

Height: 3–4' (91–122 cm)

Spread: 30" (76 cm)

Blooms: spring to fall; repeat blooming

Hardiness zones: 5–9

Rosarians have appreciated the exhibition quality of Tabris since 1983. It is frequently used around the world in rose competitions ranging from community contests to international shows.

GRANDIFLORA

The grandiflora class was created in 1954 to accommodate a new rose—Queen Elizabeth (p. 244)—which didn't easily fit into any other existing class. This class arose from crossing hybrid teas and floribundas.

There is some controversy about the name of this cluster-flowered class. North Americans call this class grandiflora while the British call it floribunda, hybrid tea type. They are tall, upright, vigorous growers with several small stems arising from the main canes. Each cane has flowers growing singly or in small clusters, with each stem long enough for cutting. The flowers are similar to, but usually smaller than, hybrid teas and are borne in larger quantities. Some varieties are hard to distinguish from hybrid teas. Use grandifloras in the same way as hybrid teas, but prune like floribundas.

Golden Girls

Other names: Queen Wilhelmina, Forever Young

Flower color: golden amber

Flower size: 4" (10 cm)

Scent: slight

Height: 3–3½' (91–107 cm)

Spread: 24–30" (61–76 cm)

Blooms: spring to fall; repeat blooming

Hardiness zones: 4b–9

Geoff Swane named this rose to honor the many achievements of Australia's sporting women.

Golden Girls was introduced in 2000. It was named by Geoff Swane of Swane's Nurseries in Australia but bred by a Canadian, Dr. Keith W. Zary of Jackson and Perkins in California. In Australia it is considered a floribunda, whereas North Americans classify it as grandiflora. Its coppery amber pointed buds open into fragrant, deep amber flowers that pale as they mature. It bears its blooms in large trusses consistently throughout the growing season. The colorful blooms contrast beautifully with the dark green, glossy foliage that is highly disease resistant.

✿ This rose tolerates cold temperatures without protection within zones 4b and 5. It may need winter protection in regions below zone 4b. In areas where snow coverage is adequate or better, pile the snow deeply around the plant as insulation. Mulch heavily around the base where snow is less reliable.

✿ At the 1999 National Rose Trial Garden of Australia, Golden Girls was awarded the Certificate of Merit for the best floribunda.

Love

T his rose was part of a group of roses developed in 1980 by Warriner of the U.S. It was released along with Honor (p. 212) and Cherish, and all three won the All-America Selection the same year, a remarkable feat. Some classify Love as a hybrid tea while others consider it a grandiflora. Either way, it is one of the most stunning roses ever developed. It bears deep crimson pink flowers with a white reverse. The dull buds open slowly into tightly packed, classic high-centered, double blooms. The reverse of the petals is bright silvery white and is well displayed when the blooms first begin to unfurl. The brightness eventually disappears as the cupped form takes shape. The thorny stems bear sparse foliage.

❀ Love has a stocky form borne from moderately vigorous branches. It tends to spread over time, but not in an aggressive manner. The foliage is moderately resistant to disease but mildly susceptible to blackspot.
❀ During a rainfall, the weight of the blooms will sometimes cause the stems to bow down to the ground. The flowers are easily spotted by rain.

Other names: none
Flower color: deep pink with silvery white reverse
Flower size: 3½" (9 cm)
Scent: light and spicy
Height: 3–4' (91–122 cm)
Spread: 30" (76 cm)
Blooms: spring to fall; repeat blooming
Hardiness zones: 5–10

Dark pink and silver bicolored roses are rare, but this variety is certainly the best of the few. It received the Portland Gold Medal in 1980.

Queen Elizabeth

Other names:
The Queen Elizabeth Rose,
Queen of England

Flower color:
medium pink

Flower size: 3½–4"
(9–10 cm)

Scent: light tea

Height: 4½–6'
(1.3–1.8 m)

Spread: 30–36"
(76–91 cm)

Blooms: summer to fall;
repeat blooming

Hardiness zones: 4–9

This rose was introduced in 1954, an important year for roses. Queen Elizabeth was unique compared to other roses, so the grandiflora classification had to be created just to accommodate it. It is one of the most widely grown and best loved roses and has received many honors, including being named World's Favorite Rose in 1979. It bears large, double, high-centered, medium pink flowers singly or in clusters. Each flower consists of 35–40 petals in a cupped form. The dark, glossy foliage is highly resistant to disease.

❀ This trouble-free rose is ideal for hedging and at the back of borders and planters. It thrives in the worst conditions. It can endure extreme heat and humidity or a bout with insects with very little assistance.
❀ Prune it back quite hard every six years or so to rejuvenate and allow the shrub to become more compact and dense. Then the flowers will bloom at eye level so you can enjoy them.
❀ Climbing Queen Elizabeth was released in 1957. It is unreliable on the coast.

*Long, sturdy stems
make it easy to
cut and display the
infinitely reward-
ing blooms.*

Tournament of Roses

Tournament of Roses is one of those roses that fit into a variety of classifications. It is considered a grandiflora in North America but a hybrid tea elsewhere. The double, high-centered flowers have an excellent continuity of bloom throughout summer into fall. Three to six flowers form a symmetrical cluster. Each flower has 35–40 petals, and the petals are varying shades of pink.

✿ Although this beautiful rose is easy to grow, it does have some drawbacks. Some growers think it is too small, and it has only average to moderate vigor.

✿ Tournament of Roses is easily blended into mixed beds and borders and is a good variety for hedging and group plantings. It is one of the best grandifloras for display and exhibition. The flower color is particularly spectacular in warm weather.

Other names:
Berkeley, Poesie
Flower color:
medium coral pink
Flower size: 3½–4"
(9–10 cm)
Scent: light and spicy
Height: 36" (91 cm)
Spread: 36" (91 cm)
Blooms: summer to fall; repeat blooming
Hardiness zones: 4–9

The name refers to the annual rose parade held in Pasadena, California. This rose was released to the public for sale on the occasion of the parade's centenary.

MINIATURE

M iniature roses are small, sparsely prickly and usually grown on their own roots. Miniatures were very popular in the early 19th century when the first miniatures, cultivars of *Rosa chinensis* 'Minima', were produced in abundance. Their popularity waned with the introduction of the polyantha roses. Interest in miniatures was rekindled when Dr. Roulet found a China rose growing in a window box in a Swiss village. This small rose was called Rouletii. Many miniature varieties were bred from Rouletii.

Most of the modern miniature roses were developed from the breeding program of Ralph Moore in California. Some newer varieties arise from other than miniature parents. These popular roses look like their bigger relatives— the hybrid teas and floribundas—but they are smaller, usually less than 18" (46 cm) tall. They bear tiny flowers and foliage.

Miniature roses are ideal for edging beds and borders, for raised beds, planters or rock gardens or for use indoors as houseplants. Climbing and trailing miniatures are also available, a result of crossing miniatures with *Rosa wichuraiana*. Patio roses, another type of miniature rose, are slightly larger than miniatures and resemble floribundas. Another type has been introduced that bears flowers slightly larger than miniatures but smaller than floribundas. They are called mini-flora. Miniatures require consistent deadheading for the best display of blooms.

Beauty Secret

Other names: none
Flower color: medium cardinal red
Flower size: 1½" (3.8 cm)
Scent: sweet and subtle
Height: 10–18" (25–46 cm)
Spread: 8–12" (20–30 cm)
Blooms: mid-season; repeat blooming
Hardiness zones: 5–11

Beauty Secret is a double, high-centered, classically shaped miniature. Upright and vigorous, Beauty Secret produces well-branched, semi-glossy foliage that forms into a neat growth habit. Strong, straight stems are tipped with cardinal red floret clusters that bloom for an extended period with little fading. The petal edges form a distinctive point. The flowers, with an average of 24–30 petals each, are sometimes borne singly but most often in clusters of four to ten.

This rose was considered the classic miniature rose of the 1960s and is just as popular today.

✿ Use this miniature in garden beds and borders, as low-growing edging and in containers. It is particularly suitable for growing indoors, year-round or just through winter.
✿ This hardy and highly disease-resistant rose is virtually maintenance free and a stunning performer.
✿ Ralph Moore developed this rose in the U.S. and it was introduced in 1965. It was awarded the first ARS Award of Excellence, in 1975. It was one of the first roses to be granted the ARS Miniature Rose Hall of Fame Award when it received that honor in 1999.

Cinderella

Though it appears fragile and delicate, Cinderella is one of the toughest, hardiest miniatures available. It is classified as a micro-mini because of its tiny, double, tightly filled, evenly rowed flowers. The pinkish blooms fade to white. Petite, semi-glossy leaves blend nicely with the colorful blossoms, creating a dainty display.

Other names: none
Flower color: white; pale pink edges
Flower size: ¾" (2 cm)
Scent: light and spicy
Height: 10–12" (25–30 cm)
Spread: 10–12" (25–30 cm)
Blooms: spring to fall; repeat blooming
Hardiness zones: 4–11

✿ Cinderella is vigorous and bushy, upright and densely compact and almost always covered in large clusters of flowers. The flowers, smaller than those of other modern miniature roses, are borne on short, twiggy, nearly thornless stems.

✿ This highly disease-resistant variety requires very little care or attention. It is always in demand by florists for use as a cut flower and by gardeners for miniature rose beds or rock gardens or as an indoor plant in winter.

✿ The color of the flowers is more crisp and intense in cooler climates.

From the time it was introduced in 1953, Cinderella has been one of the most popular miniatures. It was created by the pioneer of miniature roses, Jan de Vink from The Netherlands.

Golden Beryl

Other names: none

Flower color: bright yellow orange

Flower size: 1–2" (2.5–5 cm)

Scent: mild

Height: 12" (30 cm)

Spread: 12" (30 cm)

Blooms: early summer to fall; repeat blooming

Hardiness zones: 4–9

Golden Beryl was introduced in 1995 by one of the leading Canadian amateur hybridizers, George Mander. It bears perfectly formed blossoms that are large by miniature standards. The tiny flowers look like high-centered hybrid tea blooms. The flowers are borne atop a bushy yet compact form. The intense yellow flowers display deeper tones of orange in hot weather and locations with full exposure. The flowers emerge very early in spring and continue well into fall.

❀ This miniature works well in containers and in mixed beds and borders. It is very effective when planted en masse, as the colors tend to catch the eye of those who pass.

❀ This variety requires little to thrive and has a good level of disease resistance.

Golden Beryl is one of the best yellow miniature roses available for exhibiting in rose shows and competitions. It shows beautifully whether in a formal competition or at home in a treasured vase.

Gourmet Popcorn

Gourmet Popcorn is a sport of Popcorn and has similar characteristics but a few unique traits as well. It bears cascading clusters of rounded, white, semi-double, tiny flowers with short stems. The flowers are complemented by deep green, lush foliage. Gourmet Popcorn vigorously forms into a compact, cushion-like, rounded shrub. It really is more of a small shrub than a miniature rose.

✿ This rose is stunning planted en masse or in pots, containers, hanging baskets or any small spaces that need a boost. Gourmet Popcorn emits a distinctive honey scent. Plant this rose where the fragrance can be best enjoyed—alongside pathways, under windows or next to a garden bench.

✿ It is highly resistant to disease and virtually maintenance free.

✿ In warmer regions, Gourmet Popcorn can grow up to twice its typical height, creating a stunning specimen bearing hundreds of flowers at a time.

Other names: Summer Snow

Flower color: white

Flower size: ¾" (2 cm)

Scent: honey

Height: 18–24" (46–61 cm)

Spread: 24" (61 cm)

Blooms: summer to fall; repeat blooming

Hardiness zones: 4–9

Gourmet Popcorn won the Royal National Rose Society Trial Ground Certificate in 1995 and is frequently voted a favorite by U.S. growers.

Green Ice

Other names: none

Flower color: white, hints of pink and chartreuse

Flower size: 1¼" (3 cm)

Scent: slight

Height: 8–16" (20–41 cm)

Spread: 16–24" (41–61 cm)

Blooms: mid-season; repeat blooming

Hardiness zones: 5–11

The blooms' color intensity is greatly affected by light levels. The flowers have a deeper green tone in partial shade and fade to white with a hint of green in full sun.

The unique flower color of Green Ice is its most outstanding characteristic. Pinkish buds emerge in spring and open to double, white blooms touched with a hint of pink. The flowers then change to a light chartreuse green as they age. Green Ice is a dwarf, vigorous, low-growing shrub with a spreading form. It can be trained as a tiny climber in the right location. Glossy, dark green foliage is produced on short, lax stems. It bears hundreds of flowers during the first blooming cycle.

✿ Green Ice is ideal for cascading over rock walls and embankments. It is suitable for hanging baskets, edging or borders and blends nicely in larger garden settings. Some people find it reminiscent of a classic hybrid tea form while others think it resembles an old garden rose, displaying double, pompom-like blooms.

✿ Green Ice is generally disease resistant but requires good air circulation and regular feeding to prevent powdery mildew.

✿ This variety was introduced in 1971 by Ralph Moore of the U.S.

Little Artist

Little Artist is sometimes referred to as a 'hand-painted' miniature because the petals look as if they've been painted with brush strokes. When the buds open, the red is somewhat flecked, then the color solidifies as the flower ages, while the centers and the undersides of the petals remain creamy white, contrasting with the striking yellow stamens. This vigorous, bushy rose is almost always covered in blossoms. Short, stiff stems with medium green, semi-glossy leaves form a neat and upright growth habit.

✿ The bright flowers consistently hold their color but are most intense at the beginning of the season. The blooms are beautiful as cut flowers or dried.
✿ The plant remains low with a spreading habit, so this rose is ideal along the edges of borders and for pots and containers.
✿ It has superb disease resistance and is virtually maintenance free.

Little Artist is one of the best roses. Its semi-double, colorful florets are unusually large for a miniature rose.

Other names: Top Gear
Flower color: creamy white; flecked to solid red edges
Flower size: 1–1½" (2.5–3.8 cm)
Scent: mild apple to damask
Height: 12–18" (30–46 cm)
Spread: 12–18" (30–46 cm)
Blooms: early summer to fall; repeat blooming
Hardiness zones: 5–11

Opening Act

Other names: none
Flower color: deep red
Flower size: 1" (2.5 cm)
Scent: none
Height: 18" (46 cm)
Spread: 14" (36 cm)
Blooms: late spring to fall; repeat blooming
Hardiness zones: 4–9

Opening Act is a modern miniature, introduced in 1994 by Brad Jalbert of Select Roses. It bears rounded petals that narrow to a distinct point, giving the blooms a ruffled effect. The long-lasting, deep red blooms are suitable for cutting and arrangements.

✿ The flower trusses on a mature bush can carry 20 or more blooms in one spray, and the flowers remain on the plant for extended periods of time. This makes up for the fact that the repeat bloom is not as profuse.

✿ Prune each spring to keep the plant from becoming leggy.

✿ This rose is ideal for exhibiting in the singles class at your local rose show. Single roses are not as popular as double varieties, but Opening Act has found its following and will likely remain popular for some time.

Pink Petticoat

Pink Petticoat, an abundant bloomer, is very easy to grow. It is vigorous and is one of the larger miniature varieties available. It is unique compared to other miniature roses in that it bears hips, and large ones at that. These hips begin to form following the flowers. Ruffled, double blooms reminiscent of tiny hybrid teas are borne in creamy yellow shades with soft coral edges. Pointy, dark, shiny foliage is densely formed underneath the delicate flowers.

✿ This rose bears massive trusses of flowers made up of 50 blooms or more. It begins to bloom later in the season than most miniature roses but is well worth the wait.

✿ Miniatures, similar to larger roses, tend to lose the energy they need to bear flowers when they're not pruned carefully. Prune out deadwood and spindly canes. Good pruning practices keep diseases and pests to a minimum, allowing the plant to focus on bearing striking blooms.

✿ Pink Petticoat has won many awards since its 1979 introduction, including the Award of Excellence for Miniature Roses (ARS) in 1980 and the Miniature Princess of Show (ARS) at the Redwood Empire Rose Society Show in 1999.

Other names: none

Flower color: cream; soft coral edges

Flower size: 2" (5 cm)

Scent: mild

Height: 24" (61 cm)

Spread: 24" (61 cm)

Blooms: summer to fall; repeat blooming

Hardiness zones: 4–10

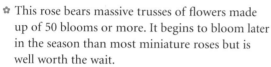

Rainbow's End

Other names: none
Flower color: deep yellow; dark pinky red edges
Flower size: 1½" (4 cm)
Scent: mild to none
Height: 12–16" (30–41 cm)
Spread: 10–14" (25–36 cm)
Blooms: early summer to fall; repeat blooming
Hardiness zones: 4–11

Rainbow's End became available in 1984 and received the ARS Award of Excellence in 1986. A climbing variety has since been introduced.

Rainbow's End is considered one of the most beautiful miniature roses ever created and is ranked the most popular miniature available today. It bears pointed buds that open into double, classic hybrid tea–type blooms in deep yellow shades touched with dark pinky red. The pinky red color will intensify in full sun, creating a distinctive edge. Age can also influence the intensity, and the entire petal may turn almost completely red. Sturdy maroon stems support small, dark, glossy leaves with burgundy, serrated edges. This rose has a rounded and compact, well-branched and upright form.

✿ Rainbow's End is one of Brad's personal favorites, one of the first miniature roses he ever grew. It must have had a substantial impact on him, since roses are now his life's work and passion. His favorite creations are miniatures, and this rose started it all!

✿ Generally resistant to disease, this rose is a little prone to blackspot.

✿ With its bushy and upright form, Rainbow's End is best in the garden. It is suitable for cut-flower gardens, beds or borders. It also works in containers or as an indoor plant in winter.

Sandalwood

The blooms of Sandalwood are russet or terracotta, one of the most intriguing colors for a rose. They display the best color when grown in dappled or partial shade. Long, pointed petals emerge in early summer and open into double, hybrid tea–like blooms. The blossoms are very large compared to other miniatures. Dark glossy foliage offsets the flowers beautifully.

Other names: none
Flower color: terracotta
Flower size: 2" (5 cm)
Scent: mild spice
Height: 14" (36 cm)
Spread: 12" (30 cm)
Blooms: early summer to fall; repeat blooming
Hardiness zones: 5–9

✿ Sandalwood is of average health and is not particularly prone to any disease. It prefers rich soil and adequate air circulation. It is a little tender in cooler temperatures, but with care it should last and perform for many years. Winter coverage may be necessary—when the days grow cool in late fall, provide an insulating layer of mulch to protect the plant.

✿ It requires only moderate pruning. Sandalwood needs optimal conditions to be successful, but it is well worth the fuss. Once you've experienced this rose, you'll do everything in your power to make it last.

Brad Jalbert, the hybridizer of this rose, claims Sandalwood is 'the most unusual and loved rose we have ever created.' A rose enthusiast in Alberta claims to have grown this miniature with great success for more than three years.

Snow Bride

Other names: Snowbride

Flower color: white

Flower size: 1½–2"
(3.8–5 cm)

Scent: slight

Height: 12–16"
(30–41 cm)

Spread: 12–16"
(30–41 cm)

Blooms: mid-season;
repeat blooming

Hardiness zones: 4–10

Snow Bride is a nicely rounded shrub and one of the best white miniatures with a hybrid tea form. This is not a rose for those who tend to neglect their plants—if it's not tended to, it will fail or become unsightly. Unlike most white miniature roses, this one consistently produces beautiful, white, weatherproof flowers. The flowers tend to be twice as large as those of other miniature varieties. The buds open into circular blossoms with pointed centers. Small, dark, glossy leaves complement the bright blossoms.

✿ This rose is suitable for containers, borders or along the edges of mixed beds. It prefers partial shade and moderate temperatures. When planted in full sun or a location with too much heat, it will become unsightly. Do not plant it where a reflection from a bright wall will intensify the heat.

Snow Bride was introduced in 1982 and won the ARS Award of Excellence for Miniature Roses only one year later.

Sweet Chariot

Sweet Chariot is well known for its sweet fragrance. It is a miniature rambler cross but has characteristics reminiscent of a polyantha. It bears small, matte foliage in medium green shades. Large clusters of loosely informal florets are borne on the stem tips. The flower color ranges from lavender to purple, aging to different mauve hues.

✿ The canes arch and spread, making this rose ideal for hanging baskets, urns and containers or as a grafted, weeping standard.

✿ It may take several weeks for this variety to begin blooming, but it is an excellent rose for any garden setting and any level of rose expertise.

✿ Sweet Chariot is very easy to grow and tolerates disease, exposure and poor soils.

Other names:
Morchari, Insolite

Flower color:
lavender to purple

Flower size: 1½"
(3.8 cm)

Scent: intense damask

Height: 18" (46 cm)

Spread: 18–24"
(46–61 cm)

Blooms: mid-season to fall; repeat blooming

Hardiness zones: 5–10

Brad notes that the flowers last much longer if kept out of the hot afternoon sun. This rose does well in partial shade with just a few hours of strong morning sunshine. In all my years of growing this rose, I have never seen a leaf with mildew on it!
— *Brad Jalbert*

Water Lily

Other names: none
Flower color:
cream with pink
Flower size: 1–2"
(2.5–5 cm)
Scent: slight
Height: 24" (61 cm)
Spread: 18" (46 cm)
Blooms: summer to fall;
repeat blooming
Hardiness zones: 4–9

Once they discover it, most people just rave about this classic rose. Water Lily is a full-bodied yet delicate-looking rose. Creamy flowers touched with pink are borne in summer and continue to bloom until fall. It is considered tall for a miniature rose, reaching 24" (61 cm) when grown in good soil in coastal conditions. The lightly scented flowers are very dense and rounded. The tightly packed petals never fully open.

❁ Water Lily sometimes bears up to 50 flowers on one stem, quite a feat for any rose. These huge sprays of flowers are more likely to be produced when the rose is grown in partial to full sun.

❁ The blooms last a long time, making this an excellent cut flower. The flowers are stunning in classic arrangements or left alone in a rose bowl. This would be the perfect wedding rose for boutonnieres and small tussie-mussies.

❁ This easy-to-grow rose requires little care, only admiration. The densely packed foliage is impervious to disease or weather.

Year 2000

Year 2000 was so named because it was introduced in the new millennium by Brad Jalbert of Select Roses. The flowers emerge yellow then change to a brilliant red from the petal edges in. The colors deepen even more in hot weather. The flowers last and last, making them ideal for cutting and crafts. The flowers are reminiscent of miniature double hybrid teas with pointed petals.

✿ This rose grows most successfully in rich soil, in partial to full sun.

✿ Year 2000 is very effective when grown in containers. If planting it in a container, use a good quality potting mix for the best results.

Other names: none
Flower color: yellow; scarlet edges
Flower size: 1" (2.5 cm)
Scent: crisp
Height: 16" (41 cm)
Spread: 12–14" (30–36 cm)
Blooms: early summer to fall; repeat blooming
Hardiness zones: 4–10

This is a great rose for the coast. The flowers are unaffected by rain. The semi-glossy, dark foliage is highly disease resistant and easy to maintain.

Resources

Gardens to Visit

Burnaby Centennial Rose Garden
Burnaby Mountain Park
Centennial Way off Burnaby
   Mountain Parkway
604-294-7450 (Burnaby Parks,
Recreation and Cultural Services)
www.city.burnaby.bc.ca

Butchart Gardens
800 Benvenuto Avenue
Brentwood Bay, BC
250-652-5256 or
866-652-4422 (toll free)
www.butchartgardens.com
email: email@butchartgardens.com

Centennial Rose Garden
624 Poirier Street
(adjacent to the Dogwood Pavilion,
   Poirier Park, central Coquitlam)
Coquitlam, BC
604-462-7249
(Contact: Corinne Brown)
www.coquitlam.ca

Horticulture Center of the Pacific
505 Quayle Road
Victoria, BC
250-479-6162
www.hcp.bc.ca
email: hcp.info@hcp.bc.ca

Kelowna Rose Gardens
1779 Rutland Road North
Kelowna, BC
250-491-7673
or 877-491-7673 (toll free)

Minter Gardens
exit #135 off highway #1
(90 minutes east of Vancouver)
52892 Bunker Road
Rosedale, BC
604-794-7191
or 604-792-3799
or 888-646-8377
www.mintergardens.com
email: mail@mintergardens.com

Park and Tilford Rose Gardens
440-333 Brooksbank Avenue
North Vancouver, BC
604-984-8200

Polson Park Rose Garden
north of the hospital between
   highway 97 and highway 6
250-542-7399
(Contact: Fred Lyall)
Vernon, BC

Queen Elizabeth Park and Gardens
33rd Avenue at Cambie Street
Vancouver, BC
604-257-8584
www.city.vancouver.bc.ca/parks/

Royal Roads University Rose Gardens
2005 Sooke Road
Victoria, BC
250-391-2511
www.royalroads.ca

Stanley Park Rose Gardens
enter from the west end of
  Georgia Street
Vancouver, BC
604-257-8400
www.seestanleypark.com/
www.city.vancouver.bc.ca/parks

UBC Botanical Garden
6804 Southwest Marine Drive
Vancouver, BC
604-822-9666
www.ubcbotanicalgarden.org

VanDusen Botanical Garden
5251 Oak Street
(Oak Street at West 37th Avenue)
Vancouver, BC
604-878-9274
www.vandusengarden.org

Rose Societies and Clubs
American Rose Society
8877 Jefferson Paige Road
Shreveport, LA 71119
318-938-5402
www.ars.org

BC Council of Garden Clubs
(represents over 125 clubs in BC)
680 Florence Street
Coquitlam, BC V3J 4C6
(Contact: Bernice Booth, President)
or c/o Lorna Herchenson,
2402 Swinburne Avenue
North Vancouver, BC V7H 1L2
604-929-5382
www.icangarden.com/clubs/bccgc
email: lherchenson@telus.net

Canadian Rose Society
17 Kintyre Avenue
Toronto, ON M4M 1M2
416-466-1879

www.mirror/org/groups/crs
email: crs@mirror.org

Fraser Pacific Rose Society
12345 – 271 Street
Coquitlam, BC V2W 1C2
or 625 Cottonwood Avenue
Coquitlam, BC V3J 2S5
604-937-3446
(Contact: Eleanor Derksen, President)
www.fprosesociety.org
email: solar@telus.net
or fraserpacificrosesociety@yahoo.ca

Peninsular Rose Club
1871 Monteith Street
Victoria, BC V8R 5X6
email: peninsular@quillserv.com

Vancouver Rose Society
c/o Bob Price
10741 Hollymount Drive
Richmond, BC V7E 4Z3
604-277-2845 (Contact: Bob Price)
www.vancouverrosesociety.org
email: bobprice@shaw.ca

Garden Centers and Suppliers
Adamson's Heritage Nursery Ltd.
1832 – 240 Street
Langley, BC V2Z 3A5
604-530-2476

Brentwood Bay Nurseries
1395 Benvenuto Avenue
Brentwood Bay, BC V8M 1J5
250-652-1507
www.brentwoodbaynurseries.com
email: bbn@shaw.ca

Classic Miniature Roses
Box 2206
Sardis, BC V2R 1A6
604-823-4884

Hardy Roses for the North
Box 2048
Grand Forks, BC V0H 1H0
604-442-8442

Old Rose Nursery
1020 Central Road
Hornby Island, BC V0R 1Z0
250-335-2603
www.oldrosenursery.com
email: oldrose@mars.ark.com

Russian Roses for the North
5680 Hughes Road
Grand Forks, BC V0H 1H4
250-442-1266
email: jlhtech-rr@telus.net

Select Roses
22771 – 38th Avenue
Langley, BC V2Z 2G9
604-530-5786
www.selectroses.ca
email: bradcan@shaw.ca

Sylvan Roses Nursery
848 Stonybrook Road
Kelowna, BC V1W 4P3
250-764-4517
www.sylvanroses.com
email: sylvanroses@telus.net

Soil Testing

Cavendish Analytical Laboratory Ltd.
1650 Pandora Street
Vancouver, BC V5L 1L6
604-251-4456
www.cavendish.ca
email: info@cavendish.ca

Griffin Laboratories Corp.
#2 – 2550 Acland Road
Kelowna, BC V1X 7L4
250-765-3399

or 1-800-661-2339
www.grifflabs.com

Island Testing Service Ltd.
Nanaimo, BC
1-800-663-7332

Integrity Sales
2180 Keating Crossroad
Saanichton, BC V8M 2A6
250-544-2072

M&B Laboratories
Units 4&5, 2062 West Henry Street
Sidney, BC V8L 5Y1
250-656-1334
www.mblabs.com
email: info@mblabs.com

Norwest Laboratories
#104, 19575 – 55A Avenue
Surrey, BC V3S 8P8
604-514-3322 or
1-800-889-1433
www.norwestlabs.com

Pacific Soil Analysis
Unit #5, 11720 Voyageur Way
Richmond, BC V6X 3G9
604-273-8226

Websites
www.everyrose.com
www.gardenwise.bc.ca
www.heirloomroses.com
www.helpmefind.com/roses
www.hortico.com
www.rosarian.com
www.rose.org
www.rosegathering.com
www.rosemagazine.com
www.theoldrosarian.com
www.weeksroses.com

Newsletter
The Rosebank Letter
Rosecom c/o Harry McGee
41 Outer Drive, London, ON
N6P 1E1
www.mirror.org/people/harry.mcgee
/rosebank.html
email: rosecom@golden.net

Reference Books
500 Popular Roses for Canadian Gardeners. 2000. Raincoast Books, Vancouver.

Agriculture and Agri-Food Canada. 2000. *Winter-hardy Roses.* Revised edition. Agriculture and Agri-Food Canada, Saint-Jean-sur-Richelieu.

Allen, Christine. 1999. *Roses for the Pacific Northwest.* Steller Press, Vancouver.

Botanica's Pocket Roses. 2001. Chief consultant William A. Grant. Whitecap Books, Vancouver.

Brown, Deni. 1996. *Roses* (an Eyewitness Garden Handbook). DK Publishing, New York.

Cairns, Thomas, Editor. 2000. *Modern Roses XI: The World Encyclopedia of Roses.* Academic Press, London/San Diego.

Druitt, Liz. 1996. *The Organic Rose Garden.* Taylor Publishing Co., Dallas.

Harrap, David. 1993. *Roses for Northern Gardeners.* Lone Pine Publishing, Edmonton.

Hole, Lois and Jill Fallis. 1997. *Lois Hole's Rose Favorites.* Lone Pine Publishing, Edmonton.

Krüssmann, Gerd. 1981. *The Complete Book of Roses.* Timber Press, Portland.

MacOboy, Stirling. 1993. *The Ultimate Rose Book.* Henry N. Abrams Inc., New York.

Moody, Mary. 1992. *The Illustrated Encyclopedia of Roses.* Timber Press, Portland.

Olson, Jerry and John Whitman. 1998. *Growing Roses in Cold Climates.* Contemporary Books (a division of NTCcontemporary Publishing Group Inc.), Lincolnwood.

Osborne, Robert and Beth Powning. 1995. *Hardy Roses: An Organic Guide to Growing Frost and Disease Resistant Varieties.* A Garden Way Publishing Book, Storey Communications, North Adams.

Phillips, Roger and Martyn Rix. 1988. *The Random House Book of Roses.* Random House, New York.

Roses for Canadians for Dummies. 2000. CDG Books Canada, Toronto.

Sammis, Kathy. 1995. *The American Garden Guides: Rose Gardening.* Pantheon Books (a division of Random House), New York.

Taylor's Guide to Roses. 1995. Revised edition. Houghton Mifflin Co., New York.

Glossary

acid soil: soil with a pH lower than 7.0

alkaline soil: soil with a pH higher than 7.0

bud union: the junction on a stem where a bud of one plant has been grafted to the stock of another

button eye (button center): the round center in a double rose blossom, composed of stamens that have turned into petals; these petals are tightly packed and cannot unfold, resulting in a button-like appearance

cane: a woody, often flexible, stem, usually arising from the base of the plant

cultivar: a *culti*vated (bred) plant *vari*ety with one or more distinct differences from the parent species, e.g., in flower color or disease resistance

deadhead: to remove spent flowers to maintain a neat appearance and encourage a longer blooming period

desiccation: loss of moisture through foliage

double flower: a flower with an unusually large number of petals, often caused by mutation of the stamens into petals

forma (f.): a naturally occurring variant that retains most of the characteristics of the species but differs naturally in some way, such as plant size or leaf color; below the level of variety in biological classification

genus: category of biological classification between the species and family levels; e.g., the genus *Rosa*

grafting: method of propagating a tree or shrub by joining a bud or cutting of a desired plant with the rootstock of another plant; the tissues grow together and top growth develops in the form of the more desirable plant

hardpan: a layer of compacted subsoil that often prevents the penetration of water or of shrub or tree roots; can occur naturally or be caused by repeated cultivation by mechanical means

hardy: capable of surviving unfavorable conditions, such as cold weather

hip: the often colorful fruit of a rose, containing the seeds

hybrid: a plant resulting from cross-breeding between varieties, species or genera; the hybrid will not breed true (yield identical offspring) when crossed with itself

inflorescence: a shoot bearing more than one flower, and usually clusters of flowers

lateral (lateral bud): bud produced in the junction between the stem and a leaf

muddled: a flower with petals that are disorganized, not forming a pattern

neutral soil: soil with a pH of 7.0

pH: a measure of acidity or alkalinity (the lower the pH, the higher the acidity); the pH of soil influences availability of nutrients for plants

pesticide: a general term for any compound used to kill insects, mites, weeds, fungi, bacteria or other pests

pith: the spongy central tissue of a stem

quilled: the narrow, tubular shape of petals or florets of some flowers

remontant: able to bloom again one or more times during a growing season

rhizome: a root-like stem that grows horizontally underground, and from which shoots and true roots emerge

rootball: the root mass and surrounding soil of a container-grown plant or a plant dug out of the ground

rootstock: the root system and lower portion of a woody plant (the stock) onto which another plant can be grafted; a vertical rhizome

runner: a modified, creeping stem that runs along the ground, forming roots and new shoots at the joints or tip

self-seeding: reproducing by means of seeds without human assistance, so that new plants constantly replace those that die

semi-double flower: a flower with petals in two or three rings

semi-hardy: a plant capable of surviving the climatic conditions of a given region if protected

sepals: leaf-like structures that protect the flower bud and surround the petals in the opened flower

single flower: a flower with a single ring of petals

species: the original plant from which cultivars are derived; the fundamental unit of biological classification, indicated by a two-part scientific name, e.g., *Rosa glauca* (*glauca* is the specific epithet)

sport: an atypical plant or flower that arises through mutation; some sports are horticulturally desirable and propagated as new cultivars

subspecies (subsp.): a naturally occurring, regional form of a species, often isolated from other subspecies but still potentially interfertile with them

sucker: a cane that sprouts from the roots or from below the bud union, therefore originating from the rootstock and different from the grafted plant

tender: incapable of surviving the climatic conditions of a given region; requiring protection from frost or cold

terminal bud: a bud formed at the tip of a stem or branch

variety (var.): a naturally occurring variant of a species; below the level of subspecies in biological classification

Index